The Deed of Words

Two Considerations on Politics of Literature

The Deed of Words

Two Considerations on Politics of Literature

Pothik Ghosh

AAKAR

THE DEED OF WORDS: Two Considerations on Politics of Literature
Pothik Ghosh

First Published 2016

ISBN 978-93-5002-330-3 (Pb)

Published by
AAKAR BOOKS
28 E Pocket IV, Mayur Vihar Phase I, Delhi 110 091
Phone : 011 2279 5505 Telefax : 011 2279 5641
aakarbooks@gmail.com; www.aakarbooks.com

Typeset at
Arpit Printographers, Delhi-110 032

Printed at
Mudrak, 30 A, Patparganj, Delhi 110 091

Contents

Acknowledgements

Every book is written by its own particular milieu. This one is no exception. However, the milieu that has written this book is no harmoniously synchronised organic community. It is, instead, a protean and, in the mind of its author, a rather fractious collective that is held together (if at all) in its contingent, shape-shifting dynamism by the Bakhtinian glue of polemical communication. It is, therefore, my ineluctable duty as the author—who is merely a persona-effect produced by the process of writing—to state how some of the key citizens of this polemical republic might have intervened in the making of this book.

Pratyush. His Hegelian emphasis on the need to remain focused on what is often fashionably rejected as historicism—especially, when we walk together as comrades in our common affirmationist search for a concrete revolutionary subjectivity—keeps me alive to the dangers of theoreticist voluntarism.

Nandini and Jesse. Their dogged insistence on negativity generates a force-field that has my affirmative dialectic poised precariously but unfailingly on the edge of the negative.

Dhruba. His rigorous articulation of "finite freedom" has taught me that an affirmation of radical finitude is, contrary to current fashions, not an abandonment of the infinity of politics in order to escape into some Arcadian and quietist world of ethics. And that an engagement with the conception of finite freedom is, instead, in some sense indispensable for affirmation of politics as emancipation of infinite thought, in antagonism to the infinite totalisation of capital and its metaphysics.

Abir. He has been a constant reminder that one cannot judge thinking merely by the ontic violence it produces.

Nazmul. Our five-year-old epistolary relationship has its basis in a shared fanatical persistence to read literature philosophically. It is a relationship that Nazmul has, more often than not, enriched with his precocious rigour and blinding insights.

Najeeb. His stubborn insistence—in our ongoing conversation of many years—to approach even the most 'formalist' works of literature and cinema in terms of a politics of experience is an unflagging source of zeal and inspiration.

Sunandan. He brought me to the doors of the wondrous universe of Akhtaruzzaman Elias more than two decades ago.

Prasanta. For putting up with my ugly truncations of literary canonicity, and continuing to see, despite that, some worth in my demotic assertions on literature and art.

Paresh and Martand. They humour my interloper's exertions on literature and aesthetics, in spite of their immersion in literary scholarship.

K.K. Saxena of Aakar Books. He continues to see my abstractions as a viable publishing proposition.

Aditya. For letting the book's cover reflect his acutely modern poetic sensibility.

Last but not least, Paramita. Her everyday life-practice is a living demonstration of how one can continuously wrest thinking from the vagaries of earning a livelihood, and how creativity is made possible in and against work. This book is dedicated to her quiet proletarian courage, and her unconditional love and comradeship.

"There are no saints of literature: nothing, even with the distance of glory and death, nothing but heretics locked up in their singular heresy, who do not want communion with the saints."

—Julien Gracq, *Reading Writing*

"...negating *and destroying* are conditions of saying Yes."

— Nietzsche, *Ecce Homo*

In Lieu of an Introduction

This book is made up of two essays on Akhtaruzzaman Elias, a radical writer of Bengali prose fiction and essays from Bangladesh, and Gajanan Madhav Muktibodh, a modernist Hindi poet and Marxist literary thinker, respectively. This is, however, not a book on Elias and Muktibodh in the sense that it does not seek to critically reflect on their respective literary oeuvres. Instead, Elias and Muktibodh function here as no more than a couple of excuses—perfect excuses I must say—to loosely pose and articulate an organisation of concepts with regard to the problematic of politics of literature.

Through these essays I hope to demonstrate that radical aesthetics and radical politics ought to be considered in terms of their 'parallelism', rather than in terms of their relationality. In other words, they must be thought not in terms of some purported ontological similitude between them, but in terms of reconceptualising the question of ontology itself as subtraction from being. We call this ontological subtraction, following Alain Badiou, "non-relational relationality". In that context, what must be emphasised is art vis-a-vis radical politics should be thought not in terms of the use of art *for* politics. It must, instead, be thought in terms of the use of politics *in* art. [In the first instance, use is meant to connote instrumentalism, while in the second instance use signifies Marx's use-value as the determinate destruction of exchange-relations and thus a determinate excess of the means/ends duality.]

Therefore, what is at stake in these two essays is to think art and its politics, and art vis-à-vis politics, in terms of Badiou's concept of subtraction. Considering that subtraction is a key concept at work in both the essays, and especially the second, all I will attempt to do here is somewhat clarify this concept in terms of the (materialist) dialectic, which is the method at work in the critique of political economy.

Does subtraction, as is often believed, render the concept of negation redundant? Far from it. Subtraction, if we faithfully attend to Alain Badiou's conceptualisation of the same, does not displace negation. It is, for him, the affirmative dimension of total negation that is concomitant with its negative dimension, which he terms destruction. That negation has till now been grasped, articulated and envisaged principally by way of overly emphasising its negative dimension—or, destruction—has meant that the affirmative dimension of negation has lost its concomitance and integrality vis-à-vis this negative dimension, only to be rendered successive and subordinate. This has obviously been on account of conjunctural reasons. However, what that has meant, insofar as the practical actuality of the materialist dialectic is concerned, is a stagiest separation of the negative dimension of negation from its affirmative one, with the former being privileged over the latter. That has, for all practical purposes, ensured that negation in its operation remain a successive seriality of destructions—which is what the successive operation of the negation of the negation in Hegel's dialectical idealism amounts to. Consequently, negation has failed to articulate itself, insofar as its practice is concerned, as total negation of the vicious cycle of alternation of negation and determination. In other words, it is unable to break free of the totalising power of the Hegelian dialectical machine, and the force-field of fetishised relationality constitutive of this idealist dialectic and its totalising power of sublation. In fact, negation when it operates in this fashion—that is, by overly emphasising its negative dimension, or destructive aspect—tends to ceaselessly reproduce the idealist dialectic and its teleological structuring. In such circumstances, negation becomes an affirmation of the reality of the force-field of fetishised relationality and identity. That, needless to say, is a situation, wherein the materialist dialectic undercuts itself.

It is such a situation that has, arguably, necessitated the Badiouian conception of subtraction as the affirmative dimension of total negation. This conception of subtraction does not dispense with destruction, which is the negative dimension of total negation. All it seeks to do is diminish the excessive stress placed on the negative dimension, or destructive aspect, of total negation in order to theoretically restore concomitance, even indivisibility, of the two dimensions of total negation in its determinate operation.

Clearly then, subtraction is a conception of ontological excess in its practical operation or realisation. This ontological excess is materiality because it is the determinate emerging of the lack in a situation, and is thus the emerging of the non-anteriority of the idea that is determinately realised in that situation as the idea of the situation. It ought to be mentioned here that this reality of ontological excess—which we could also alternately term the reality or necessity of contingency—is what the Marxian critique, as the articulation of its method of materialist dialectic as the determinate operation of total negation, performs, and thus presupposes, at the theoretical level of abstraction. The thinking of ontological excess simply means thinking the practical actuality of the process of uninterrupted excess of all identities and/or teleologies as its own form. More precisely, what this amounts to, is thinking how determinate exceeding of a form, identity or destination can, in practice, anticipatively exceed the form, identity, and/or destination it will tend to yield even before that second form, identity, and/or destination has actually been yielded.

What such thinking of ontological excess—as thinking the practical actuality of the process of uninterrupted excess of all forms, identities, and/or goals—amounts to is not, as is often believed, the jettisoning of dialectical thinking. Instead, what it clearly demonstrates is thinking the dialectical structure in order to anticipatively exceed, and extenuate, it. It is to think the dialectic concretely in terms of its determinate asymmetry or antagonism—rather than the other way around; think the determinate asymmetry in the dialectic in terms of the dialectic in its abstraction. This is precisely what distinguishes, and radically at that, the materialist dialectic from the idealist Hegelian one.

Now, to think the determinate excess of a form, identity, and/or destination anticipatively exceed, in practice, the form, identity, and/or destination it will tend to yield on account of being that determinate excess in the first place, even before that second form, identity, and/or destination has actually been yielded, is an eminently valid theoretical possibility. But one that would be an absurdity, insofar as its realisation in practice as such is concerned, and which would, therefore, retroactively render its thinking or theorisation solipsistic, and open to infinite regress. Unless, of course, one thinks of such practical realisation in terms of a historically concrete construction that in being (in a present-continuous sense) that construction seeks to actually, as opposed to potentially, articulate the determinate unravelling of the force-field of fetishised relationality, and the sublationary power of the idealist dialectic that is constitutively realised in the historically concrete factuality of that force-field. The concept of subtraction, or subtractive ontology, is understood here precisely in terms of such a construction as its own being. We now clearly see how subtraction, as the affirmative articulation of total negation in its practical actuality, does not do away with the destructive dimension but, instead, renders that dimension the integral antagonistic force of the construction that this construction in its determinate being articulates with regard to the force-field of fetishised relationality in its historically concrete factuality. More pointedly, destruction is the force that subtraction in being itself wreaks on the structure of exchange and relationality that tends to foil this ontological subtraction. As a result negation, thanks to its affirmative articulation as subtraction, ceases to work as a contradiction to emerge in its full antagonistic glory.

After all, the structure of exchange relations—or the force-field of fetishised relationality—by its very presence tends to ensure that the event is always already lapsed. The event being the determinate emerging of the lack in the structure of exchange-relations in its historical factuality. Or, which is the same thing, the structure tends to subsume determinate moments of subtraction—or its determinate excess or determinate antagonism—by re-articulating them in order to reproduce itself as that structure by recomposing itself historically. The structure of exchange- relations is, therefore, itself the very power that impedes its immanent asymmetry—which, as a result, drives that structure to reproduce itself through expansion—from coming into its own as subtraction in its sustained being. In such a situation, the truth of an event —which is determinate excess of, or antagonism to, the structure of exchange-relations—can be sustained only when it generalises itself as the subtraction it is. And it can generalise itself thus only when destruction, which is the negative dimension of total negation of which such subtraction is the affirmative dimension, is integral to subtraction so that its sustained being spells destruction of the obstructionist structure. There is no subtraction if destruction, or the negative dimension of negation, is not integral to the former in its articulation. And what would, in such circumstances, go under the name of subtraction would actually be a kind of ethical withdrawal, or opting out.

Of course, the construction we have mentioned above is nothing but this sustained being of subtraction in its practical and historical actuality. And to that extent, this construction involves a subjective decision. But this decision, which as its own actuality is the construction in question, is not teleologically orientated and thus its character is not decisionist. Instead, this decision has a rather strange character. It is, to put it more accurately, a wager, precisely because it is a decision that seeks to realise the impossibility of decision. In other words, it is an intentionality of the impossibility of intentionality. Or, it is an intentionality that is orientated towards the possibility of non-intentionality and is, therefore, intentionality as its own displacement. The subjectivity that embodies this decision or intention—or rather, the subjectivity 'interpellated' by such a decision and intention—is, to draw on Badiou yet again, a "subjectivity without a subject". Hence, the construction in question would be a movement that is not teleological. In fact, precisely because it is an adventure, which is a movement that is dispersive and thus non-teleological, is it truly a construction and not speculation. This constructionist adventure in its practical actuality would be subtraction in its historicity. It is this constructionist adventure, and nothing else, that is materiality.

Therefore, subtraction, as the conception of affirmative articulation of total negation in practice, is a conception of the practical actuality of antagonistic negativity of the dialectic. It is, as Badiou appositely terms it, "political negativity". Unlike ontological difference, subtraction is not about nonbeing entering the mode of being, rather it is in-existence as a process. This gives us a conception of a radically distinct order of ontology, which Badiou has rather pithily characterised as "nothing as something". This "nothing-as-something" is subtraction-from-existence as ontology. In other words, while ontological difference, pace Heideggerian authenticity, is thought in terms of nonbeing entering the mode of being, we could say that ontological subtraction (or subtractive ontology) must be thought in terms of being under the condition of nonbeing. That is precisely the reason why the thinking of ontological difference amounts to the abandonment of dialectic *tout court*, while the thinking of ontological subtraction impels one to ask, 'what is the limit that separates an idealist dialectic from a materialist one?'; and to, therefore, think the conditions under which a dialectic is materialist.

The actuality of ontological subtraction, to speak about it illustratively with regard to the political domain, is the real movement that is the free association of direct producers. As the ceaselessly perpetual movement that is the free association of direct producers—and one which is, therefore, radically separate from a movement that is successively continuous—it is also simultaneously an articulation of destructive antagonism vis-à-vis the force-field of fetishised relationality in its determinate factuality, and the infinitely totalising sublationary power of the idealist dialectic this force-field incarnates. Ontological subtraction articulates a destructive antagonism with regard to the force-field of fetishised relationality, and its constitutive contradictoriness, because it is relationality under the condition of the nonrelational. Simply put, ontological subtraction would, in its actuality, be nonrelational relationality as an uninterrupted process. And it is this that is materiality; the materiality of encounter.

The Insurrection of Akhtaruzzaman Elias

Politics of Literature and Elias' Savage Mind

The question of politics with regard to an artist or a litterateur is usually encountered and understood in terms of what position the artist or the litterateur in question strikes as an individual with regard to the political situation of his day. The terms of such understanding, more often than not, also extend to what he says about politics in his works of art or literature. That is the dominant approach to the question of an artist or a writer's politics. We could call this the question of literature in politics or politics in literature—the problematic of art/literature about politics, or the problematic of political art. This is, without doubt, a valid approach in dealing with the question of art and politics, and their relationship. However, what one is more interested in here, through this attempted engagement with the works of Bangladeshi writer Akhtaruzzaman Elias, is another approach. An approach that has arguably come down to us from Marx——evident in his engagement with the literature of Classical Hellenic Antiquity—through, primarily, Walter Benjamin and Bertolt Brecht. (There have, of course, been others like Adorno and Ernst Bloch, and such Althusserians and post-Althusserians as Pierre Macherey and Jacques Ranciere respectively, not to forget Fredric Jameson, who have adopted one or another variant of this approach in their engagement with art and literature.) This approach seeks to deal with the question of art and politics in terms of what we ought to call 'the politics of art'.

What does this approach entail? It seeks to deal with art and literature not principally in terms of what artistic or literary works have to say on or about politics, but what is the politics they pose by virtue of being the works of art or literature they are. More precisely, this approach attempts to grasp the politics posed by the aesthetics of the works in question. That is, it tries to grasp the politics of a work of art or literature by figuring out the organisation of space constitutive of that work. This approach attempts to unearth the politics of art in terms of how the question of relationality has been embodied by the text of a work of art or literature, and envisaged in its production. For, it is the logic of relationality that is constitutive of the organisation and structure of space thus giving that structure and organisation a specific character, whether in our so-called real, social life or the life of the world that is a novel, a story, a poem, a painting or a film. It is this character of the structure or organisation of space of a work of art that is its economy, while that which founds this character or economy and/or renders it manifest is its politics.

The two approaches of dealing with the question of art and politics delineated above are not mutually exclusive. They are interdependent. However, the stress here, in dealing with the question of politics with regard to Elias's literature, will fall principally on the latter approach. That is not to say one intends to evade engaging with Elias's works in terms of the former but one certainly wishes to understand how what Elias says about politics in and through his literary works derives from the politics his literature as such speaks. That is, how it is actually the politics of Elias's literature which renders what that literature says on or about his contemporary political situation, and on politics in general, complete and effective. It might be a repetition to once again explain and explicate the terms of the approach and concept of politics of literature. But it might not be a bad idea to do so, perhaps at some length, before we begin engaging our determinate object—that is, the literary works of Elias. On that score, Ranciere (2011, pp. 3-4) provides us with an apposite conceptual compass:

"The politics of literature is not the same thing as the politics of writers. It does not concern the personal engagements of writers in the social or political struggles of their times. Neither does it concern the way writers represent social structures, political movements or various identities in their books. The expression 'politics of literature' implies that literature does politics simply by being literature. It assumes that we don't need to worry about whether writers should go in for politics or stick to the purity of their art instead, but that this very purity has something to do with politics. It assumes that there is an essential connection between politics as a specific form of collective practice and literature as a well-defined practice of the art of writing.

"....Politics is the construction of a specific sphere of experience in which certain objects are posited as shared and certain subjects regarded as capable of designating these objects and of arguing about them. But such a construction is not a fixed given resting on an anthropological invariable. The given on which politics rests is always litigious. A celebrated Aristotelian formula declares that men are political beings because they have speech, which allows them to share the just and the unjust, whereas animals only have a voice that expresses pleasure or pain. But the whole issue lies in knowing who is qualified to judge what is deliberative speech and what is expression of displeasure. In a sense, all political activity is a conflict aimed at retracing the perceptible boundaries by means of which political capacity is demonstrated. Plato's *Republic* shows at the outset that artisans don't have the time to do anything other than their work: their occupation, their timetable and their capabilities that adapt them to it prohibit them from acceding to this supplement that political activity constitutes. Now, politics begins precisely when this impossibility is challenged, when those men and women who don't have the time to do anything other than their work take the time they don't have to prove that they are indeed speaking beings, participating in a shared world and not furious or suffering animals. This distribution and this redistribution of space and time, place and identity, speech and noise, the visible and the invisible form, what I call the distribution of the perceptible. Political activity reconfigures the distribution of the perceptible. It introduces new objects and subjects onto the common stage. It makes visible what was invisible, it makes audible as speaking beings those who were previously heard only as noisy animals.[1]

"The expression 'politics of literature' thereby implies that literature intervenes as literature in this carving up of space and time, the visible and the invisible, speech and noise. It intervenes in the relationship between practices and forms of visibility and modes of saying that carves up one or more common worlds."

Now the question is: what is the politics of Elias's literature? It is, we ought to contend, insurrectionary. And that is exactly what this essay intends to demonstrate. To be more accurate, it must be said the politics posed by Elias's literary aesthetic is insurrectionary. In fact, one should further qualify one's take on Elias by contending the politics that the aesthetic—or more precisely the aesthetic economy—of his literature renders evident is insurrectionary, as opposed to being merely insurgent.

Before we proceed any further we would do well to clarify what insurrectionary politics is and how exactly is it to be distinguished from what one has chosen to term insurgent politics. Insurrection is generalisation of the emergent logic of a localised moment of insurgency—which is doubtless its constitutive moment—through the overcoming of that localisation into multiple insurgent moments that erupt uninterruptedly and simultaneously.

But how does this politics of insurrection manifest itself in aesthetics, the aesthetics of literature to be precise? Elias's literature—his two novels [*Chilekotar Sepai* (*Soldier in the Attic*) and *Khowabnama* (*Dream Chronicle*)] and over two dozen stories —is an apposite instantiation of the same. The organisation of the space of his literature—which is its aesthetic—is constitutive of what Levi-Strauss terms "the savage mind". It is on account of such constitutivity that the politics of Elias's literary aesthetic becomes insurrectionary. According to Levi-Strauss (1966, p. 245), "The savage mind totalizes" and "it is in (the) intransigent refusal on the part of the savage mind to allow anything human (or even living) to remain alien to it, that the real principle of dialectical reason is to be found".

The French anthropologist further clarifies the principle of dialectical reason—and thus the savage mind—when he takes issue with Sartre's *Critique of Dialectical Reason* to explain and explicate the relationship between analytical reason and dialectical reason. He writes (1966, p. 246): "...the opposition between the two sorts of reason (analytical and dialectical) is relative, not absolute. It corresponds to a tension within human thought which may persist indefinitely *de facto*, but which has no basis *de jure*. In my view dialectical reason is always constitutive: it is the bridge, forever extended and improved, which analytical reason throws out over an abyss; it is unable to see the further shore but it knows that it is there, even should it be constantly receding. The term dialectical reason thus covers the perpetual efforts analytical reason must make to reform itself if it aspires to account for language, society, and thought; and the distinction between the two forms of reason in my view rests only on the temporary gap separating analytical reason from the understanding of life. Sartre calls analytical reason

reason in repose; I call the same reason dialectical when it is roused to action, tensed by its efforts to *transcend* itself."

After all, a new analytic of thinking emerges as the subjectivity of an object to critically overcome externalised determination, and the meaning imposed on it through representation by an already existing analytic subjectivity so that the object can free itself from the violence done to it by the latter analytic, which is nothing but the abstraction of its own prior subjectivity. This, in order to assert itself in its concreteness. That is, to affirm itself as its own subject: Badiou's "subjective-materiality".[2] (2009, p. 198)

As a result, the unconscious of the analytical mode of reason is to overcome all analytic abstractions, including itself. The savage mind is the generalisation or awakening of this unconscious of analytical reason with the latter self-reflexively grasping itself as the former.

Therefore, the savage mind is activation of dialectical reason, which is analytical reason constantly overcoming itself by grasping its own logic of emerging to actualise it. The logic of emerging of analytical reason is, it must be stated at the risk of some repetition, also its unconscious when it exists as itself, which is dialectical reason in "repose". Clearly, the savage mind is constitutive of the process of the self being transfigured into its beyondness. Therefore, as the actuality of the principle of dialectical reason it is de-identitarianising and cannot, therefore, have its locus ontically fixed in a self. Levi-Strauss puts that across quite succinctly when he writes: "I do not regard dialectical reason as *something other than* analytical reason, upon which the absolute originality of a human order would be based, but as *something additional* in analytical reason: the necessary condition for it to venture to undertake the resolution of the human into the non-human."

And insofar as the savage mind is constitutive of the critical overcoming of externalised determination and analytical abstraction, it posits a critique of duality and relationality on one hand and identity principle on the other. The savage mind can, therefore, also be envisaged in terms of affirmation of singularity and non-identity. The savage mind can, therefore, be construed as a figure of the actuality or historicity of singularisation or counter-totalisation of infinitely different space-times. A historicity of singularity as it were.

It must, however, be stated here as an aside that one has absolutely no intention of upholding the methodological structuralism of Levi-Strauss's anthropology. In horizontalising various historical phenomena into an ethnography of relativised laissez-faire in terms of the universality of the deep structure that, according to the French anthropologist, constitutes them, this structuralism shares a methodological affinity, insofar as its political effects are concerned, with a kind of deontological and thus ahistorical Kantianism. This problem, it must be stated here in passing, stems from the theoretical level of abstraction being collapsed on to the practical or existentially-lived level of determination. A move that conceptually renders the subjective operation of dialectical thinking directly correspondent to and fully commensurate with the dialectical constitutivity of the structure (structural dialectic) in its objectiveness.

What the argument here takes from Levi-Strauss is basically his conceptualisation of the "savage mind" as a mode of social being animated by, and constitutive of, the operation of dialectical thinking. That not only serves to explicate the singularising and insurrectionary politics of Elias's literature, it also arguably enables one to find the resources, from within Levi-Strauss' anthropological discourse itself, to critically break with the crisis of structuralist relativism—a schizzed conception —that animates his ethnological method and discourse. That becomes possible on account of this conceptualisation of the "savage mind" being premised on the explicit recognition of the dialectic between history and structure (or logic). One that, in Benjamin's words, enables us to brush history (as in its historical analytic) against its own grain (the dialectical logic of its emerging). Only a mind that counter-totalises— that is to say, seeks universalisability of the singular—is inhuman, monstrous and thus truly savage. The totalising mind is merely an abstraction of the mind as a counter-totalising process. It is, therefore, as that abstraction, a phantom-double of the the counter-totalising mind. One that Levi-Strauss locates only, however, by mistaking the phantom for the real. In having the phantom stand as the real, the French anthropologist ends up posing the caricature of the savage mind as the real thing. And yet, this caricature is important as it, in drawing attention to its own phantom-ness, reveals the real it seeks to conceal and substitute for.

This counter-totalising savage mind—which is Levi-Strauss' totalising "savage mind" brushed against its own grain—both singularises infinitely diverse spatio-temporalities and is, therefore, simultaneously also their singularity. And it is this counter-totalising savage mind that is rendered rather explicitly evident in a constellation of different space-times of resistance that Elias constructs in his *Chilekotar Sepai* (2000, pp. 187-188). Those different spatio-temporalities come together in and as the unity of their moments of insurgent, and thus evental, emerging to palpably inhabit, in the eyes of protagonist Osman Gani, a protest march on the streets of Dhaka against the Pakistani occupation of East Bengal:

> *Yesterday Ayub Khan's police killed a boy from the university, such a huge protest happens, Anwar can't get to see any of it! ...Osman's heart skips a few beats: so many people here, are they all breathing, fish-rice-eating normal human beings like him? This human flood here, he finds the attire, demenaour of many of them unfamiliar? Who are they? Does it mean, people from eras long gone by have also joined the procession? Here see, smack in the middle of the procession are short dhoti-clad denizens of Dhaka from the time of Islam Khan's reign! In fact, those who would, in an even earlier time, travel to Sonargaon and back in*

boats full of sacks of rice have come too. Inhabitants of Bangla Baajar and Tantibaajar (weavers' market) have emerged from the frozen heart of the vanished canal to come here? Here are the turbaned soldiers, from the time of Ibrahim Khan's reign, who were killed in a skirmish with Prince Khusro. Osman gets a start on seeing those who died of hunger in Shaiyasta Khan's Dhaka of the time of eight-maunds of rice for a taka. They have had nothing to eat for 300 years, —their steps in harmony, they march ahead with their black hair fluttering in the breeze like a wave. People battered by the Mughals, people battered by the Mogs, people battered by the Company's merchants—could this procession have been this big had everyone not turned up? The Maratha priest has emerged from the dry layers of bricks of the Racecourse Kali Temple to come down here swinging the falchion, Majnu Shah's fakirs are here too, here go the nuslin weavers throwing and waving their thumb-torn fists in the air, their eternally black bare bodies roast in the sun. Today, the naked, starving, skeletal bodies of weavers who weave taka 4,000- worth jamdanis walk an erect walk. The imams, muezzins, musullis of Babubajar Mosque riddled with bullets by the British are marching ahead, instead of muttering verses from the Quran they roar today, 'We shall not let it go in vain!' Here come the soldiers of Lalbagh Fort, mangled by the beastly bites of insatiable desire of Nabab Abdul Gani, Ruplal, Mohinimohon, let loose by the red-faced sahibs. Sepoys of Meerut have torn away the nooses around their necks to come down from the palm trees of Victoria Park, sepoys of Bareilly, sepoys of Swandeep-Sirajganj-Goaland. No dear, even that doesn't suffice. The mother-worshipping youths of Jugantar and Anushilan in their dhotis and vests are coming, in their midst the two murdered boys of Kaltabajaar can be separately identified. From below the Naarinda bridge comes Somen Chanda, the bloody wave of Dolai canal on his head. There, that is Barkat! His skull has been blown off. That, at first sight, frightens Osman a little but he quickly takes hold of himself. So many people! In the high tide of a new water Dhaka's past and present are today overflowing and dissolving into one another, today its morning-afternoon-evening-night are forgotten and stand dissolved, today the city is without its east-west-north-south, all the signs that divide and distinguish the seventeenth-eighteenth-nineteenth-twentieth centuries stand erased. Today, the city of Dhaka is fully intent on occupying this limitless time and space. Osman's heart trembles: how far will he be able to go with this massive deluge? How far? Like a quaking pitcher under the running tap at the mouth of Golok Pal Lane becomes

> *still once it is full to the brim, our Osman Gani's heart too has gradually become full and complete, by becoming one of the smallest molecules of this uninterrupted tidal surge he is experiencing a warmth in his heart. That is no mean recompense? With his heart full he throws his fist in the air and roars, 'Will not let it go in vain.'* (My translation.)

Clearly, what the historical-sociological specifications or mediations of those struggles are—that is, their identities—do not seem to matter in this novelistic depiction. At any rate, it is a secondary concern. Instead, what the discourse of the novel seeks to bring to the fore is the universality that each of those struggles in their mediational specificity posit. Each of those struggles in the specificity of being ranged against their respectively particular historical domination posit the unconscious of overcoming the general condition of externalised determination, and thus duality and relationality. It is this singularising unconscious, which can also be called the unconscious of universal-singularity, that is actualised in this passage from *Chilekotar Sepai* through the construction of this constellation that is accorded the reality of an existentially-lived world or space-time. This constellation is, therefore, nothing but the world of the savage mind—the savage mind in its own space and time.

Insurrection as Popular Culture, or from the Subaltern to the Oppressed

This example—typical of Elias's literary aesthetic of the savage mind, and thus its insurrectionary politics—is, among other things, the enactment of popular culture. The discourse constitutive of such an aesthetic enables us to discern in it a conception of culture that is the singularising and singular configuration of space-times. It affirms a politics of culture that can, following Raymond Williams, be termed "cultural materialism". Following his literary aesthetic, we could say that Elias, not unlike Williams, envisages culture as the materiality of life, wherein this materiality of life is not the positivist abstraction of that empirically-lived life. Instead, real materiality of life, for militant-intellectuals like him and Williams, emerges only when the living of life is a mode of struggle and self-critique. This aesthetic seems to suggest that popular culture, as Elias would grasp it, is not the discursive appearances of forms of subaltern expression that identitarianises culture. Rather, it would, for him, be precisely the expression of an impulse—of course made possible as that expression through the mediation of forms and their historically and sociologically given discursive resources—that tends to overcome the identitarian logic and politics of culture. On the other hand, culture is an embodiment of identitarian logic and politics when it is grasped in terms of its formal stability and discursive abstraction. This latter sort of culture should—following the insurrectionary aesthetic vision embodied in and by the discourse of Elias's novels and stories—be comprehended as nothing but culture as the logic of representation, identitarianisation and domination. This, for us, is, clearly, culture as a commodity and ideology, and thus culture as the politics of capitalism.

In the Eliasian scheme, which can be discerned from the nature of the writer's literary aesthetic, popular culture would be the historicity of flow and flux beyond formal abstractions —which nevertheless exist, but now as images of the constitutive moments of such flow and flux because it is only in and through their predications that determinate instantiations of the nonidentitarian flux occur. Popular culture would, for Elias, be the actuality of force of the flow that unravels its own formal fetishes, which are tendentially inevitable, to overcome the centripetalising regimentation that compels it to turn into culture as bourgeois domination, and thus also into an embodiment of its politics of hegemony (in a precise Gramscian sense). Thus popular culture would, for Elias, be the expression of the generalisation of the tendency of de-representation, de-identitarianisation and centrifugalisation. Insurrection is nothing but the generalised expression of such a tendency, which in and as that generalisation is the actuality and historicity of nonidentity and singularity. Clearly, for Elias, culture is truly popular only when it seeks to actualise or embody the minor.

In the novel *Khowabnama*, for instance, the actuality of the centrifugalising force in its singularity is broached through the opposition posed by the mediations of the paganised-heretical Islamic discursivities of wandering mendicant and minstrel Cherag Ali's traditional canon of mythic stories and anonymous Delphic dream-reading riddles, songs, limericks and doggerels to the sociology and discursive appearances of the culture of the dominant class of rich kulaks such as Sharafat Mandal, which has a relatively more orthodox Islamic religious dimension. The historical sociology of this opposition, more precisely contradistinction, is envisaged in the novel to reveal the unconscious of the heretical cultural discursivity and its concomitant subaltern sociology. And that unconscious of the sociology and discursivie identity of the subaltern culture, by virtue of it being constituted thus in its bid to overcome the domination and externalised determination by the dominant culture, is to obtain to the condition of singularity. After all, the sociologically relational existence of those two discursive appearances of culture proves the discursive appearance and sociology of the subaltern culture has constituted itself as what it is—that is, in its difference from the discursive phenomenon and sociology of the dominant culture—to thwart being represented, determined and thus dominated by the latter. By that same token of its logic of emerging it must, therefore, also overcome itself as that culture of subalternised discursive phenomenon and sociology, which renders it an identity precisely and simultaneously in being the difference it is.

The novel in question reveals that unconscious, or incipience, of the heretical-subaltern sociology and discursivity of Cherag Ali's culture by actualising it, precisely by having that culture-as-difference (read difference-as-identity) overcome and transfigure itself. The constitutivity of mystic-mendicant Cherag Ali's culture, which is subtractive and singular, is shown in the novel to actualise itself through its unfolding by overcoming, and in the process transfiguring, the discursive predication of Cherag Ali's thought. Such overcoming and transfiguration sustains the actuality of the centrifugalising force in its singularity, which is popular culture, by preventing its hypostatisation into a sociology or artefact of so-called popular culture. And that happens through the reconstitution of the centrifugalising force, which was constitutive of Cherag Ali's discourse in its moment of emerging, in and through the new songs of social criticism and revolutionary transformation composed and performed by his self-appointed disciple Keramat Ali in the high-noon of the Tebhaga movement. What is at stake here is clearly not the actuality of the two cultural or discursive forms. It is not about the phenomenal difference registered by the latter form with regard to the former in mutating from it either. What is, instead, at stake, as far as the emphasis of the novel at this point is concerned, is the actuality of the mutation itself. In other words, what is being staked out here through the two discursive, cultural or sociological phenomena and their difference is the actuality of the simultaneity of difference and the deployment of that difference. The novel demands that we focus here not on the actuality of phenomenal difference but on the actuality of deployment of difference that the emerging of difference as a discursive phenomenon—in the latter (Keramat Ali's discourse) mutating from the former (Cherag Ali's discourse)—registers.

The break constitutive of the transfiguration of the figure of Cherag Ali into that of Keramat Ali produces, to talk in an Althusserian language, two different forms of "historical individuality" (Balibar; 1999, p. 252). But these two historical individualities, or figures of discourse, are different not merely in terms of the two sociologically different ontic positions they occupy. Nor, therefore, is the difference between the two limited to the different discursive appearances of their respective discourses: anonymous mythic doggerels on one hand, and avowedly self-composed songs of social transformation on the other. Rather, what sets the two individualities radically apart is the break between their respective modalities of discourse, which marks an epistemological rupture in the qualities of the orientation of their respective subject-positions. Something that makes them inhabitants of not only two different historical situations but two radically different historicities or epochs. It is precisely on account of this difference that the two figures faithfully bear out the Althusserian concept of "historical individuality".

The novel in having Keramat Ali assert that he is a disciple of Fakir Cherag Ali, even while he explicitly abandons the discursive pattern of the latter's discourse, makes him into an active subject of his own production as the singular centrifugalising force by reconstituting it through and as the new discursivity of songs of social transformation. It reveals that Keramat Ali is aware he is reclaiming the singular centrifugalising force, constitutive of the subalternised sociology and appearance of Cherag Ali's discourse in its moment of emerging, in precisely abandoning the phenomenal heritage of that discourse. This, therefore, also implies that, unlike the sociological figure of Cherag Ali, the sociological figure of Keramat Ali is reflexive in his awareness of the unconscious of the historically specified discourse he determinately produces. The way he has been envisaged in the novel implicitly indicates his awareness of the need to also overcome the sociology and discursive phenomenality of his own discourse—which he has produced in the process of overcoming the sociology and discursive appearance of Cherag Ali's discourse—in order to maintain his fidelity to the singularity of the centrifugalising force.

So, while the historicity and sociality constitutive of the sociological figure of Fakir Cherag Ali are respectively that of duality and identity, the historicity and sociality constitutive of the figure of Keramat Ali, which are also the historicity and sociality posited by the novel, go beyond the historical sociology of Keramat Ali to be the historicity and sociality of singularity and nonidentity. The former is a figure of anti-capitalism that is constitutive of the epoch of capital. The latter, on the other hand, is a figure of the communist epoch. It must, however, be stated here that precisely because the historicity that Elias's novel *Khowabnama* constitutes is singular, do we encounter Cherag Ali not only as the sociological self he is, but also as a figuration of subjectivity beyond that sociologically specified, existential self of his. That figure is animated by the character of the spectre of Cherag Ali, who appears even after the death/disappearance of his sociologically-specified existential self. This clearly instantiates the radicalisation of the empirically-lived, sociologised finitude of a character such as Cherag Ali by transfiguring his existentially-limited and sociologically-specified present into a perpetually open present by stretching that existentially— or empirically-lived finitude in its very moment to that of infinite beyondness. The doubling, or tripling, of the figure of Cherag Ali—in and as the characters of existentially-lived Fakir, his spectre and his self-appointed disciple Keramat Ali—symptomatises his finitude in its inhumanly monstrous radicalisation. This savagely insurrectionary spatio-temporality is the novelistic space of *Khowabnama*, insofar as that novelistic space is constitutive of the inhumanity of such monstrous radicalisation of the existentially-limited human finitude.

The transcending of the self-other binary—by bringing the self and the other into a constellated unity of, what Badiou would term, "the singular-multiple" (2010, p.82) by abolishing the dualising relationality among them—is precisely what such doubling (or repetition or twinning) of character-figures accomplishes. Such constellated transcending of that binary is a recurrent motif in Elias's literature. It is echoed, for instance, by most of his stories that are enactments of the singularising interplay of different, psychotically estranged alterities of otherwise consolidated selves. The devices and registers of subtraction,[3] which are so integral to Elias's literary discourse, enable the enactment of such singularising interplay of alterities. They are dream [Laalmiya and Bullet in '*Jaal Sopno, Sopner Jaal*'(The Dream-web and Counterfeit Dreams')]; violently idiosyncratic reverie [Osman in '*Pratishodh*' (Revenge), Romij Ali in '*Keetnashoker Kirti*' (Feat of the Pesticide)]; eccentric recalcitrance [Mobarok Ali in '*Apaghat*' (Mishap), psychotic break [Haddi Khijir and Osman Gani in *Chilekotar Sepai*, Abbas Pagla and Mili in '*Miliir Haatey Stengun*' (Mili and Her Stengun), Nurul Huda in 'Raincoat']; intoxication [Samarjeet in '*Khonwari*' (The Alcoholic Stupor)]; and schizophrenic meditation on self and history [Ronju in *Nirrudesh Jatra* (The Unknown Journey)].

These examples—and especially *Khowabnama*—serve to demonstrate that in Elias's creative prose the practice and discourse of the subalternised subject-positions are not championed as such in terms of their sociology and discursive abstractions. Rather, they are affirmed in terms of their singular/singularising logic of emerging. This, the discursive appearance and sociology characterising their subaltern 'identity', in its difference from the identified (or identitarianised) discursivity and sociology of the dominant culture, mediately indicates. Such affirmation is, as the example from *Khowabnama* demonstrates, integral to the reclamation of the singularity by critically overcoming precisely that identified and identitarianised discursive appearance and sociology of subaltern culture. This, among other things, implies that for Elias subaltern cultures in the mere finitude of their difference do not denote popular culture. The former do not amount to the latter in its uninterrupted and infinite openness. Subaltern culture as difference instantiates, at best, the repetition of the succession of infinite finitudes, wherein finite freedom as withdrawal from the horizon of infinite totalisation is really no more than subjective illumination that only serves to accelerate the reproduction of the identitarian horizon of infinite totalisation at the objective level.

A subalternised culture is objectively coeval with popular culture only in its evental moment or moment of emergent constitutivity. And in that moment the culture in question is neither identity, nor its subalternity, but precisely the determinate instantiation of the nonidentitarian excess of the structure within which they are produced as identity and its subalternity. This nonidentitarian excess, needless to say, immbolises the metaphysical dynamic of that ontological structure, while simultaneously also interrupting the differentiating flight from it that only serves to return and reproduce that structure.

To grasp the sociologies and discursive appearances of the culture of subalterns in such terms is to realise that justice can be done to the popular grain of those cultures only by critically overcoming them in their subalternised existence. Grasping and actualising such internal critique posited by those subaltern cultures due to the fact of their differential existence vis-à-vis the identity of dominant culture, is considered indispensable by Gramsci for an effective and meaningful project of Marxist sociology.

Through his criticism of Nikolai Bukharin's *Theory of Historical Materialism: A Manual of Marxist Sociology*, which is shown to be lacking on that score, Gramsci (1996, pp. 419-420) demonstrates why and how the sociological discursive appearances of subaltern cultures must be grasped in terms of their own singular constitutivity of emerging, and thus their own internal critique. This they themselves posit as their own unconscious or negativity. He articulates his criticism of Bukharin thus:

"The first mistake of the ***Popular Manual*** is that it starts, at least implicitly, from the assumption that the elaboration of an original philosophy of the popular masses is to be opposed to the great systems of traditional philosophy and the religion of the leaders of the clergy—i.e. the conception of the world of the intellectuals and of high culture. In reality these systems are unknown to the multitude and have no direct influence on its way of thinking and acting. This does not mean of course that they are altogether without influence but it is influence of a different kind. These systems influence the popular masses as an external political force, an element of cohesive force exercised by the ruling classes and therefore an element of subordination to an external hegemony. This limits the original thought of the popular masses in a negative direction, without having the positive effect of a vital ferment of interior transformation of what the masses think in an embryonic and chaotic form about the world and life. The principal elements of common sense are provided by religion, and consequently the relationship between common sense and religion is much more intimate than that between common sense and the philosophical systems of intellectuals.... In common sense it is the "realistic", materialistic elements which are predominant, the immediate product of crude sensation. This is by no means in contradiction with the religious element, far from it. But here these elements are "superstitious" and acritical...."

It, therefore, follows that the sociological specificity of subaltern culture establishes its own specific identity precisely in the moment it tends to differentiate itself from the sociology and discursive appearance of the dominant culture in its identified and identitarianised specificity. The assertion of discursive specificity by a subaltern culture in order to differentiate itself from the particular identity of a dominant culture is intrinsic to its attempt to obviate its representation and domination by the latter. However, the assertion of such differentiating identity presupposes the condition of duality—for, difference, in order to affirm itself, needs to assert and exist in its discursive particularity with regard to a specific identity from which such assertion is meant to affirmatively distinguish it. And this condition of duality and relationality is constitutive of competition, domination and representation. This condition is the condition of possibility of the mutually interdependent existence of domination and competition. Hence, a particular form of domination cannot be truly abolished without simultaneously abolishing competition and the condition of possibility of their mutually constitutive existence in general. It is precisely for this reason that a subaltern culture, even when it exists as such through the assertion of its difference vis-à-vis the identity of a dominant culture, continues to be dominated, and even *represented,* in terms of the very discursivity it asserts to affirm its difference, by the dominant classes and their cultural systems. Clearly, the assertion of a subaltern culture as the index of affirmation of difference vis-à-vis a dominant culture spells the abolition of neither the latter as the specific identity it is nor the relationality of domination it co-founds.

In that context, the attempt by a subalternised people to rid themselves of their subordination by the dominant class through the assertion of their culture—that is, their specified way of life—reveals itself to be governed by the very condition of possibility of domination. For, the assertion of difference with regard to identity, as we have seen, posits the structure of duality that is this condition of possibility of identitarianisation and domination. In such circumstances, this struggle of the subaltern against its subordination through the assertion of the differentiating specificities objectively amounts to no more than competition, which co-founds domination and is thus simultaneously co-constitutive of duality as their condition of possibility. That is exactly what Gramsci implies when he writes about "the popular masses" and their "original thought" being subordinated "to an external hegemony" of "the great systems of traditional philosophy and the religion of the leaders of the clergy", even as such "conception of the world of the intellectuals and of high culture...are unknown to the multitude and have no direct influence on its way of thinking and acting".

What this suggests is that the existence of a way of thinking and culture specific to the subalterns ("original thought of the popular masses" in Gramsci's words), in spite and because of its particular difference that sets it apart from the specified identity of the thought of the dominant classes by differentiating it from the latter, is still determined or articulated by its structuring logic. Being subjected to such hegemony means that not only does the subordination of the differentiating specificity of subaltern culture by the culture that has identified and established itself as dominant not cease in spite of the affirmation of the former as difference, but also that this difference in being affirmed as such is rendered a subordinate cultural form or identity that itself turns into a dominant material force with regard to other strata that it simultaneously produces through its own internal recomposition and differentiation. The production of such strata, through that process of internal differentiation and recomposition of the 'original' subalternity, is coeval with the variation of the discursive resources constitutive of that culture-as-difference-as-identity so that those strata come to acquire the discursive markers of their respective cultural specificities that also serves to designate their respective social status.

Gramsci (1996, p. 420) lays this process bare in this note on Bukharin: "The principal elements of common sense are provided by religion, and consequently the relationship between common sense and religion is much more intimate than that between common sense and the philosophical systems of intellectuals. But even within religion some critical distinctions should be made. Every religion, even Catholicism..., is in reality a multiplicity of distinct and often contradictory religions: there is one Catholicism for the peasants, one for the *petits-bourgeois* and town workers, one for women, and one for the intellectuals which is itself variegated and disconnected." *Khowabnama* further elucidates this process when it shows how Islam, which is the religious-cultural and, eventually also political, expression of the subordinate social status of rich kulaks such as Mandal and his Muslim Leaguer son Abdul Qader, vis-à-vis the upper-caste Hindu absentee landlords and their Congress backers, is itself internally differentiated into a paganised-heretical Islam of landless peasants, poor sharecroppers and fisherfolk. That is so because the relatively more orthodox Islam—which is doubtless a marker of both subordination of kulaks like Mandal by the upper-caste Hindu culture of the absentee landlords, and thus also the competitive struggle of the former against the latter—is, however, in relation to the social strata of those believers of paganised-heretical Islam, a discursive cultural marker of the material force of domination that is constitutive of such differentiation of the Muslim identity in the part of East Bengal where the novel is set.

There should, however, be no doubt that the orthodox variant of a kulak's Islam would instrumentalise the heretical Islam of the poor and the landless if the latter fail to grasp the self-critique unconsciously posited by their difference in its predication by the particularity of their religio-cultural differentiality. A self-critique whose actualisation would lead to that heretical religio-cultural difference overcoming both itself as the identity it becomes in asserting itself as that difference, and thus also the social differentiation and the politics of competition that are its conditions of possibility. It is through such overcoming of itself that a subalternity grasps and transforms itself into a figure of the oppressed as it occurs in Marx. This process of transformation of a subalternity into the Marxian figure of the oppressed, through the critical unravelling of itself as the identity it becomes in asserting its difference, entails that this identity self-transformatively grasp the domination it experiences in the particularity of its historical situation as the operation of political force as simultaneously both dominance and hegemony, which tends to repress and decimate singularity. This is the hidden fact of oppression that the figure of the oppressed through its reflexively embodied realisation brings to light.

As a consequence, it envisages its struggle against the historical particularity of the domination it experiences as the universal affirmation of singularity in the very finitude of that historically and sociologically particular domination. It is this that makes such struggle, at once, both world—and self-transforming. Thus the struggle of a dominated people who grasp themselves as the figure of the oppressed is a dialectically articulated struggle that is simultaneously directed both against their domination in its immediate historical particularity, and exploitation and duality, which comprise the mediated generalised condition of possibility of such domination. The figure of the oppressed in its reflexive realisation and concomitant struggle is, therefore, a figure of the critique of political economy in its actualisation. It is, by that same token, also the figure of revolutionary subjectivity, and its actuality in and as revolutionary praxis, that Marx designates as "class-for-itself".

But the problem is that the bearers of particular and particularised subordinate cultural identities do not experience the specific relationships of domination, which results in them acquiring those identities, as part of a larger, totalising historical-social process. Marx (1986, p. 817) says as much while criticising "vulgar economy" for affirming and "feel(ing) particularly at home in the estranged outward appearances of economic relations". That, according to him, "does no more than interpret, systematise and defend in doctrinaire fashion the conceptions of the agents of bourgeois production who are entrapped in bourgeois production relations". This impels him to conclude that "all science would be superfluous if the outward appearance and the essence of things directly coincided".

Nevertheless, implicit in this otherwise sound formulation of Marx is the fact that the science of general and generalised essence of exploitation is the synthesis of the infinitely open totality of historical experiences of different dominations. In such circumstances, the oppressed as the actuality of its politics would be the embodied concentration of that science of generalised exploitation into the finiteness of a particular experience of domination. It would be the realisation of the general and generalised infinity of different historically specific experiences in the finitude of that existential particularity. Clearly, through such reflexive realisation of the oppressed, the Marxist science of critique of political economy fulfils itself by being restored to and dissolved into the experientially marked phenomenality of finite existence, thereby becoming the actuality of revolution as a singular sequence of politics. It is this restoration of science to experience, which accords to science the hallmark of Nietzschean gaiety, that the generality of science and the particularity of experience are short-circuited to be transfigured into the universal-singularity of praxis. Elias accomplishes precisely that in his literature. The constitutive deployment of the affective registers and tropes of psychotic break as subtraction—either as characters or situations, or both —in almost all his novels and stories serve to manifest the critical science of generalised singularity in and as the affectivity of experience. We could call this literary discourse of Elias his gay science.

And the above example from *Khowabnama*, which reveals precisely that, is no exception to the gay scientificity of his discourse. It attempts to show how the Tebhaga movement, by virtue of being a movement of radical transformation of inegalitarian agrarian production relations, is enabling the margin of margins to grasp this differentially particularised identity of theirs in terms of the unconscious self-critique they posit. The actualisation of such self-critique begins to enable, as the novel demonstrates, the identity of the margin of margins (not in the deconstructive sense ascribed to it by Ajit Chaudhury but in a literal sense) to overcome and transfigure itself and, therefore, in the same movement also move towards abolishing the stratified and differentiated socio-economic order that is its condition of possibility. But the novel also shows how the retreat and eventual collapse of that movement—thanks to the withdrawal of its Communist leadership for the sake of Hindu-Muslim amity in undivided Bengal and the rest of India—leads to the instrumentalisation of the pagan-heretical Islamic cultural identity of the landless peasants by the relatively more orthodox Islamic identity of the kulaks such as Mandal and his son Qader in the service of the Muslim League demand for the partition of undivided Bengal. An indisputable example of hegemony-reinforcing competitive politics of a subordinate people—Islam being the identity of the common struggle of landless, middle and rich peasants—against the dominant absentee landlords, whose specifying cultural identity is by and large upper-caste Hindu.

Yet, the fact remains that it is precisely such competitive struggle of the subalternised people against the particular form of their subordination by the dominant classes that posits the unconscious will of such competition to overcome itself and its constitutive condition of possibility (duality). This unconscious is posited by virtue of its striving to stop being dominated, and thus represented and identified, in its immediate particularity.

That is clearly symptomatised by its exertion to establish its own particular identity—in the process of differing from the dominant cultural, and thus political, identity as a move to beat the latter's representative imposition—through the assertion of a specifying discursive phenomenon and sociology to affirm its difference. But as long as this unconscious is not grasped for what it is, and generalised—which would lead to the creation of a qualitatively new historical and social actuality; the insurrectionary historicity and sociality of the savage mind—the struggle of the subordinated against the dominant is doomed to remain a struggle against the particular kind of domination the former directly encounters and experiences. This would obviously amount to no more than the assertion of a specific cultural and political identity by the subordinated against the cultural and political identity of the dominant in the particularity of their historical and sociological situation. As a result, it would, precisely in being the struggle that it is against domination, cancel itself out by being the vehicle of the very hegemony of the logic of domination and its identitarianising and dualising condition of possibility that it is implicitly directed against. It must be said here that this perpetuation of hegemony by the struggle of the subordinated masses against their domination is not on account of the fact that it wages such a struggle—which is clearly inescapable and necessary—but it is so because of how that struggle is thought and envisaged in its limited particularity.

Gramsci indicates that when he insists the "external hegemony" of "the great systems of traditional philosophy and the religion of the leaders of the clergy", which "the original thought of the popular masses" are subject to, "limit" that thought of the popular masses "in a negative direction, without having the positive effect of a vital ferment of interior transformation of what the masses think in an embryonic and chaotic form about the world and life". Hence, the only way for the subordinated masses to rid their culture and its politics of the hegemony they are subjected to is through their reflexive grasping of the unconscious will of such culture to non-representation, nonidentity and singularity, thanks to the constitutive logic it posits in its moment of emerging through the assertion of what can be called a differential identity with regard to the discursively specified identity of the dominant culture. Something that its subjection to hegemony prevents, leading it to simply assert itself as a 'differential identity' vis-à-vis the discursively-specified identity of the dominant without simultaneously critiquing its own assertion of that differentiating identity in order to actualise the essential grain —or unconscious—of such an assertion. It is this grasping of its unconscious will to singularity and nonidentity by a discursively-specified identity of subaltern culture—in the process of overcoming itself as that identified (or identitarianised) discursive appearance—that Gramsci terms the "interior transformation of what the masses think in an embryonic and chaotic form about the world and life".

Therefore, when the Italian militant and philosopher states that in "common sense it is the "realistic", materialistic elements which are predominant, the immediate product of crude sensation", he is effectively arguing that common sense is an analytic of thinking that emerges as the subjectivity of an object to critically overcome externalised determination, and the meaning imposed on it through representation, by an already existing analytic subjectivity. This subjective emerging occurs, as has been observed earlier, for the object to free itself from the violence of abstraction perpetrated on it by an already existing analytic, and assert itself in its concreteness. But precisely because it does not self-reflexively grasp this logic of its own emerging it ends up replacing one analytic abstraction, that of great systems of traditional philosophy and high culture, with another, that of common sense. And that is precisely why, according to him, the elements of common sense "are here 'superstitious' and acritical".

While criticising Croce and Gentile's understanding of common sense in this note on Bukharin, Gramsci (1996, pp. 422-423) characterises common sense as "...the naïve philosophy of the people, which revolts against any form of subjectivist idealism, or... (it is) good sense and a contemptuous attitude to the abstruseness, ingenuities and obscurity of certain forms of scientific and philosophical exposition".

That, however, does not suffice for Gramsci. He knows that common sense—which is the cultural-system of thought of the "popular" or subaltern, masses—fails to engage in its own critical overcoming. A self-critique posited as its unconscious, which can be discerned from the discursively indicated fact of it having been constituted in opposition and difference to the traditional philosophy of the leading classes. For him, common sense is the necessary but not sufficient condition of possibility for the emergence of popular culture. He clarifies that by having his "methodological" stress fall on "starting from a critique of common sense...(does) not mean that the critique of the systematic philosophies of the intellectuals is to be neglected". He also adds, "Indeed, because by its very nature it tends towards being a mass philosophy, the philosophy of praxis can only be conceived in a polemical form and in the form of a perpetual struggle." He then qualifies that by arguing that "none the less the starting point must always be that common sense which is the spontaneous philosophy of the multitude and which has to be made ideologically coherent". Gramsci clearly demonstrates that something more than sheer common sense is needed for popular culture to be actualised in its full insurrectionary glory. It means that common sense, or whatever other identified and identitarianised forms and sociologies of culture of the subalternised masses there are, must simultaneously seek to critically overcome themselves even as they constitute themselves as those discursively-specified forms in their difference and/or opposition to the identities of cultures that are dominant in relation to them in the respective particularity of their historical situations.

The Gramscian Moment in Elias and His Crude Thinking

A similar critical spirit and approach with regard to the sociologies and discursively-specified forms of cultures of the subordinated, the marginals and the subalterns is evident in Elias too. Like the Gramsci we have just encountered, Elias is also not at all concerned with such sociologies and discursive appearances of cultural forms as such and in themselves. He, in striking contrast to many petty-bourgeois radical intellectuals and artists of his modern South Asian and Bengali milieu, is arguably not enamoured of such sociologies and forms of subaltern and marginal cultures. Hence, unlike them, he also does not believe in romanticising such sociologies and discursive appearances of forms of marginal and subaltern cultures. He is, instead, interested in those sociologies and discursive forms, and is drawn to them, precisely because they—by virtue of being characteristic of particularisingly 'differential identities' of subaltern cultures vis-à-vis identified cultures of the elite and the dominant—posit their unconscious will to singularity and nonidentity by tending to critically unravel, supersede and transfigure themselves as those cultural discursive identities and sociologies of subalternity. Such an approach is not only rendered evident by his literary aesthetic—something that we have already seen through examples from his novels, especially *Khowabnama*—but is also evident in his theorisation of culture and its politics. In an essay, Elias (2000, pp. 12-13) writes:

> *The community of lower-class working masses has been the home of some of the recent Bangla novels. Some writings have even managed to effectively bring out their misery and deprivation. In poetry, exploitation of the lower classes has been dealt with, and resolutions to participate in*

> *the struggle for emancipating them from such exploitation have been declared. Such literary and artistic productions have conscientised many boys from lower-middle-class and middle-class families. They have shed middle-class beliefs and petty aspirations to walk the rough road of leftist politics. But in none of these literary and artistic productions is the culture of the lower classes brought to fruition. Then how can I, in these cases, accord anything more than the prestige of still photographs to the reflections of lower-class life found in them?* (My translation.)

This excerpt is representative of the deep aversion he nurses for the propensity among petty-bourgeois radicals to valorise sociologies and historical forms of subaltern and marginalised cultures as such. Sociologically and discursively-specified forms of culture of the marginal and the subordinated are, for Elias, no more than hypostatised artefacts of popular culture. It is for this reason that he critically designates such cultural forms - which he finds manifest in the representation of the lives of subalternised people in much of contemporary Bangla art and literature—"still photographs of lower-class life". According to him, such congealed and abstracted moments—still shots—of the life of the popular masses do not manifest and realise popular culture. What he implies here is that the existence of the artefacts of subaltern culture, which are nothing but abstracted and hypostatised moments of popular culture, symptomatises the failure of the singular constitutivity of those artefacts in their moments of emerging (which is thus also their singularising unconscious) to generalise and actualise itself by overcoming and unraveling precisely those artefacts.

The conception of popular culture posed by Elias in this essay is one that articulates such culture as an uninterrupted movement from localised insurgency to generalised insurrection in the process of having the truth of singularity of the former in its evental moment of eruption extend itself by preempting the abstracted fetishisation of the form that informs its instantiation as the determinate overcoming of social mediation, precisely by having that abstracted form brush itself against its grain.

This, therefore, means that Elias has no intention of jettisoning those artefacts of discursively-specified practices and discourses of subalternity—which is cultural difference-as-identity. However, he does not consider them significant in themselves either. For him, their only significance is their potential capacity to accomplish precisely what those artefacts of subordinated culture have failed to do on account of their romanticised identitarianised existence. For Elias, the importance of those identitarianised artefacts of subaltern culture lies in the self-historicising and self-critical unconscious they posit by virtue of their specific historical situation and position, which is highlighted through their discursive specificities. And they become, as we have already seen through some examples, indispensable resources of Elias's literary discourse, wherein they are articulated precisely as symptoms of their self-critical unconscious. It is on account of such radical functioning of those artefacts and discursive forms of subaltern culture in Elias's literary discourse as its constituent elements that such discourse is an instantiation of the aesthetic of the savage mind and its politics of insurrection.

This self-historicising, self-critical radical functioning of discursive appearances and forms of subordinate cultures in Elias's literary discourse as its indispensable constitutivity is nothing but the singularising mode of "crude thinking" at work. Brecht seeks to propound this mode of thinking—which he calls dialectical as opposed to the undialectical modalities of high philosophical thinking—by affirming such non-conceptual registers of commonsensical mass discourse as adages, proverbs, folklore, fairytales, rhymes and doggerels. He is once supposed to have famously remarked: "Nothing is more important than learning to think crudely. Crude thinking is the thinking of great men." But what Brecht hails, when he affirms those non-conceptual, commonsensical discourses, is not those discourses in their immediate discursive appearances or identities, but the modality of thinking constitutive of those discourses that their discursive appearances render accessible.

Such discourses emerge in and as the articulation of resistance of non-specialist thinking of the common masses against the abstruse modality of high-philosophical thinking, and its esoterically specialised and thus conceptually systematised discourse that tends to dominate, objectify, identify and identitarianise. The specifying discursive patterns of the former discourse, in indicating its difference with regard to the latter, reveal that. It follows, therefore, that the logical tendency of thinking constitutive of such commonsensical mass discourses in their emerging is de-identitarianising and de-representational. Hence, the modality of thinking constitutive of such common and mass discourses in their crude, non-systematic and non-systemic registers militates against the tendency of representation, discursive abstraction, identitarianisation and domination. To that extent, the mode of crude thinking is also the self-critique its constitutive common, non-systemic discourses posit as the unconscious of their own discursive abstractions. It is this that makes crude thinking—cognate with Levi-Strauss's savage mind as analytical reason "tensed by its efforts to transcend itself", or Gramsci's philosophy of praxis as common sense in autocritique—a dialectical, singularising and singular modality of thought.

Elias, not unlike the crude-thinking Brecht, disdains the high-philosophical modality of thinking, constitutive of conceptually systematised registers of discourse, for its propensity to produce dead abstractions estranged from feelings, emotions and the affectivity of experience. He (2000, pp. 14-15) writes:

> *Man is not merely an ingredient of history. Or, man is not merely an equipment to establish some theory. The working people are makers of history. Their lives cannot be explained and understood in theory....* (My translation.)

And this disregard for high theory, especially the conceptually articulated theoriations of revolution and socialism, figure continually in his literary discourse. Such scorn for the mode of high philosophical thinking arises off and on in both his novels, especially *Chilekotar Sepai*, and many of his stories, as unsparing statements of ridicule directed at the register of high theory and culture, and their mostly upper-middle-class and middle-class social location. Often, this ridiculing of high theory, especially its radical variant, is realised in his literary discourse through ironical descriptions of, or sarcastic comments on, the sociological detail of the lives of its upper-middle-class and middle-class purveyors. In Elias's accurate estimation, that is a phenomenon symptomatic of the alienation of the culture and idea of radical politics from the experiential affectivity of the subalternised working people. The following excerpt from his (2000, pp. 211-212) story '*Utsob*' ('Festivity') makes for a telling example:

> *When either Muntasir, or Ishtiaq, or Aaharaar come, conversations on socialism in soft dulcet tones ensue even as they play Kanika Bandyopadhyay's LP. Again, amid all this what sweet pain of loneliness is suffered. And when that happens there is nothing to be done save listening to Duke Ellington for two full hours with the air-conditioner running while the ceiling fan is turned on at its fullest.*
>
> *And see here! In the dead of night eight-nine dogs are running around – from this end of the alley to that. Aren't there dogs there? They are there too. There was one, a gentleman, at the wedding reception. What a solemn expression the gentleman had, what physique! With what majesty he stood there mildly wagging his tail. It seemed as if a gentlemanly landlord, just like in a Bangla film, is sitting on his balcony in a deck-chair rocking himself while enjoying the sunset. When you see such dogs a feeling of devotion is bound to be aroused in the soul.* (My translation.)

Such examples seem to suggest that Elias's politics of discourse is anti-theory. And that he, like most other modern radical petty-bourgeois intellectuals and artists from South Asia, is in the business of degrading and rejecting theory to romanticise and sociologise the life of the common masses in the name of some authenticity of experience. Nothing, however, could be farther from the truth. If we do a close reading of the essay, which has been cited here in bits and pieces, we will realise the error of such an inference. The last cited passage itself, when read in its entirety, reveals that. Even as Elias argues that man is "not merely a useful ingredient for the establishment of a theory", and "that the way of life of the working people cannot be explained with the aid of theory", he also makes it a point to state that the meaningfulness of art is derived from it being the search for the deep truth of life amid the working people's way of living and practice of culture. He (2000, p. 15) goes on to add:

> *Only through such a process of inquiry can the truth immanent in theory be revealed. Art and literature is not about proving things, in there inquiry and theoretical principles move together, they are contiguous with one another, it does not do to show one by tearing it away from the other.* (My translation.)

This declarative statement by Elias implies that like a classical crude thinker, he is also equally negatively disposed to the practice of experiences estranging their registers of emotion and feeling from thinking thus becoming hypostatised and reified in their discursive appearances into discourses and practices—i.e. cultures—of common sense and massified belief.

It also indicates that Elias's rejection of the modality of high philosophical thinking is certainly not meant to spell a romanticised celebration of discursive abstractions of discourses and practices of the so-called common people, dwelling in their massified passivity, as popular culture. He is, after all, as averse to theory alienating itself from the consciousness of felt living, as the practice of affectively experienced living alienating itself from thought to be reduced to custom and belief. The following excerpt from the essay (2000, p. 9) in question bears that out:

> *...the cultural practice of the lower classes is not witnessing any development, after having reached a particular stage its evolution has virtually come to a halt.... Their practice of culture has, in trying to move from its current stage to a new level, been stumbling.* (My translation.)

What this reveals is that Elias does not consider sociologies and discursive appearances of the culture of marginals and the subordinated as such to be popular. For him they were popular culture in their respective moments of insurgent emerging and will once again be so when their insurgent constitutivity, or tendency of their emerging, is generalised and actualised into the insurrectionary historicity of singularity.

Therefore, his rejection of the culture of high philosophical thinking is meant to be an affirmation of, what can, following Benjamin (1998, pp. 159-235), be called the allegorical principle of theory, and its politics. And it is this allegorical principle of theory that Elias enacts as the authorial subject of his literary discourse.

The Literature of Practical Consciousness and its Allegories of 'Command'

As a writer of creative prose, he faithfully adheres to this allegorical principle of theorising. That is evident in his desire—symptomatised by the operation of his literary discourse—to grasp theories and concepts in and as the affectivity of the respectively different experiences of living them in their formation, and thus grasp those affects in the singularity of their instantiations as feelings of experiencing the formation of theoretical discourses in their emerging. This affective living of discourses in their formation is to experience, what Williams calls, their "practical consciousness" (2010, pp. 130-131). Such consciousness, Williams (2010, p. 131) writes, is "...what is actually being lived, and not only what it is thought is being lived". What is, however, even more crucial for us is what the

British literary thinker (2010, p. 131) says by way of further elaboration of that concept: "Yet the actual alternative to the received and produced fixed forms is not silence: not the absence, the unconscious, which bourgeois culture has mythicized. It is a kind of feeling and thinking which is indeed social and material, but each in an embryonic phase before it can become fully articulate and defined exchange. Its relations with the already articulate and defined are then exceptionally complex."

Clearly then, to experience that affect of living a discourse in and as the moment of its non-discursive formation, or emerging, is precisely not to contemplatively reduce it to its discursive appearance but to grasp the singularity of living it in its formation through the affective experience of such living. The singularity thus grasped—by virtue of its modality of grasping through living the grasped—is demonstration as a concept, and not concept as discursively encoded knowledge. This demonstration as concept, wherein a form is rendered accessible as the demonstration of its own theory, radically changes the status of the concept. Now, concept, as far as the realm of practice is concerned, is no longer discursively-encoded knowledge functioning as a normative directive vis-à-vis practice. Rather, concept, or theory, in being its own demonstration, is, as far as the realm of practice is concerned, a command that is there to be heeded without, however, being compulsively imposed. This is what allegory, in its specifically Benjaminian sense, arguably amounts to.[4] Thus, this radically altered status of the concept (its allegorical status) is, in contrast to its traditional normative status, all about the concept being a command without being a directive. More precisely, the status of the concept is that of a command that is, at the same time, not a directive. We ought to call this concept-as-command, or a command-concept.

We call it so because it is a concept that 'commands' us to repeat the practical living of singularity, and affectively experiencing it as such, by overcoming precisely that discourse, whose formation one lived and experienced affectively to cognitively grasp the command of singularity. It must be added here that this singularity, which is cognitively grasped by experiencing the affectivity of living discourses, ideas and practices in their emergent formation, is what Williams (2010, p. 132) conceptualises as "structures of feeling". He (2010, p. 132) explains: "The term is difficult, but 'feeling' is chosen to emphasize a distinction from more formal concepts of 'world-view' or 'ideology'. It is not only that we must go beyond formally held and systematic beliefs, though of course we have always to include them. It is that we are concerned with meanings and values as they are actively lived and felt, and the relations between these and formal or systematic beliefs are in practice variable (including historically variable), over a range from formal assent with private dissent to the more nuanced interaction between selected and interpreted beliefs and acted and justified experienced." He (2010, p. 132) then goes on to add, "We are talking about characteristic elements of impulse, restraint and tone; specifically affective elements of consciousness and relationships: not feeling against thought, but thought as feeling and feeling as thought...."

It is, therefore, not surprising that dreaming is one of the principal registers of thinking and theorising history in Elias' literary discourse. The experience of dreaming, as opposed to the knowledge of dreams one acquires after waking up from dream, is one of the key devices of psychotic break constitutive of Elias's literary discourse. His literary discourse represents the working of this allegorical principle of theorisation through the psychotic disposition of the characters and the organisation of the literary space such dispositions are constitutive of in his novels and stories. Thereby, the discourse itself also becomes a performative demonstration of the allegorical principle of thinking. In being what it represents in the discourse it is, Elias's literature becomes an allegory itself.

In Elias's literary discourse, dream, not unlike the other registers and devices of psychotic break constitutive of it, is not its abstracted discursive appearance or identity. Rather, it is the experience of dreaming as subtraction from, or overcoming of, the determination by wakefulness. For, when one dreams one does not know one is dreaming but experiences the dreamworld as the only reality that follows no rule of human wakefulness and normalcy and is completely free of the governance by such rules. Dream gets made sense of and identified as dream only when one wakes up. The cognition of singularity—which this dream experience enables through the end of the affectivity of living it as reality in waking up from it into its identified knowledge—gets posed as a command for reclamation of singularity. It is a command that can be followed only through the generalisation of singularity beyond the existentially-limited discursive identity that mediated the pre-wakeful dream-experience into being. This would be the practice of being singular by becoming it and thus also concomitantly living the affective experience of such being as becoming.

Dream experience ends, as we have seen, in wakefulness to inhabit its horizon of duality or binary as a constitutively alienated and subordinated identity. Similarly, experiences of insurgent (or evental) experiences of popular culture end with the beginning of history, or more precisely the historical, to inhabit it as myths. The project articulated by Elias' literary discourse is to transfigure wakefulness, sanity and history into the singularity posed in cognition by the dreaming-experience, the experience internal to what is identified and seen from its outside as madness, and the pre-mythic insurgent moment of formation of what will eventually become myth. Such experiences are singular because in subtracting from, or overcoming of, the externalised determination of wakefulness, sanity and history, and in concomitantly being their own ground and meaning, they reject duality and relationality. By that same token, they also pose the critical overcoming of their own discursively-specified and/or sociologically-identified mediating forms. Such allegorised actuality of the experiences of dreaming, insanity and popular pre-mythic insurgency would, in being generalised, be constitutive of its own historicity, which is historicity of singularity. Revolution is nothing but this condition and situation of singularty as its own historicity.

Let us now return to *Khowabnama* as an example of how the device and affective register of dream enables the allegorical articulation of Elias's literary discourse with regard to history. Let us, for instance, look at how he (1998, p. 9) begins the novel:

> *The place where Tamijer Baap (Tamij's Father) had planted his feet a little and had been waving his coal-black hands to chase away the ashen-grey clouds by standing erect to look up as much as was possible by stretching the veins of his neck, that place must be carefully considered. Once upon a time when, forget Tamijer Baap, even his father had not yet been born, it would even be a long time before his grandfather Baaghaad Majhi came into the world, one is not even sure whether Baaghaad Majhi's grandfather or the father of his grandfather had been born or not, and even if he were born he would be merely crawling around on the freshly-laid mud floor of the yet-to-be constructed house whose foundation had just been laid after clearing of the forest. On an evening of one of those days Munshi Barkatullah Shah, in order to be part of Majnu Shah's entourage of innumerable fakirs headed for the Mahasthan Fort, was headed towards Korotowa when he was killed by a bullet from the gun of Taylor, the chief of the White soldiers, and fell from his horse. The hole the bullet had made in his neck did not ever close. Once he had died, he, with chains around his neck and with his ash-smeared body, climbed on to the top of the pankur tree on the northern head of the Katlahaar marsh, and sat there with a pair of iron tongs, which had a fish engraved on it, in his hands. Ever since, during the day, he is spread out all over the marsh as sunlight within the sunlight, and all through the night he rules*

> *the marsh from the top of that pankur tree. Only if a glimpse of his could be caught—that is the hope with which Tamijer Baap waves his hands to chase away the clouds in the sky.* (My translation.)

The ashen-grey clouds that Tamijer Baap tries to chase away are his historical present, which is the eve of the Tebhaga movement, within which lives its past—the defeated Fakir-Sanyasi rebellions of the 18th-19th century among others, for instance. This past lives within his historical present as its constitutively subordinated and contradictory identity (or difference-as-identity). This is the past-as-defeat—experienced and lived as myths and beliefs by poor landless peasants and fisherfolk like Tamijer Baap, who are the bearers of this past in the dominant historical present as its difference. And precisely for that reason is this subalternised difference simultaneously also a subordinated identity. Tamijer Baap attempts to chase away those clouds of his historical present because that present obscures the experiencing of its past, when it was its present in and as its own emerging, by dominating and identifying it as the past. By chasing away those clouds of his historical present he wants to experience that past when it was present as its own emerging. That is, before it became identified as past. He wants to experience and live the past before it became identified as such through its subjection to the historical present. This chasing away of the clouds by Tamijer Baap is, therefore, a gesture to be in an open present, which is a present that does not itself become or produce a past. Following Derrida (1994, pp. xix-xx), we would do well to term this present, present without presence.[5]

And since his existential self inhabits the historical present, Taamijer Baap can access past-when-it-was-present-as-its-own-emerging through his dreaming self that in subtracting itself from the governance of wakefulness of the reality of the historical present becomes an allegorical figure of its own singularity, and thus a command-giving concept to generalise that experience of living the singularity beyond the empirical threshold of that past as it exists in its identified form determined by the historical present in question. What this simply means is that Tamijer Baap is an allegorical figure, whose existence functions as a command for reconstituting the evental experience of insurgency—as lived, for instance, during the Fakir-Sanyasi rebellion against the oppression of British colonialism—in and through the new historically mediated experience of oppressive agrarian production relations of 1940s Bengal. Not unlike Benjamin's (2003, p. 395) Robespierre, who cited Ancient Rome for the French Revolution by blasting it out of the linearly hierarchised continuum of history to grasp it simultaneously in its own present and his, Tamijer Baap is envisaged as a similar figure who cites the 18th-19th century Fakir-Sanyasi rebellions against British colonial oppression for the Tebhaga movement in 1940s Bengal. As a matter of fact, he not only cites but is also simultaneously the citation of those rebellions for his own existentially-lived historical present to generalise the evental singularity of those rebellions in their moment of lived emerging. Here is an example (Elias; 1998, p. 178) of how Tamijer Baap functions as an allegorical figure of singularity, and thus a command-giving concept for the generalisation of singularity by tearing the historical present asunder:

> *Tamijer Baap is, however, completely quiet. He looks towards Cherag Ali with the same sleepy eyes, his eyes give Kulsum an eerie feeling, does this man sleep with his eyes open, is he seeing grandfather's face in his sleep? But sleep gets the better of Kulsum's fear and prevents it from congealing, is the man smearing Kulsum's eyes with sleep from where he sits at the other end of the mat? When Cherag Ali starts singing, Kaalaam Majhi says, 'Hey you, Tamijer Baap, why the hell are you drowsing? Go home'. Yet, the man continues to sit where he is. The way his still eyes are stuck on Cherag Kulsum feels as if that man is seeing her grandfather in a dream. What kind of a man is this man? Unmoved, he sits dreaming amid so many people? Or is it that Kulsum herself is*

> *dreaming? That may be so. Otherwise how come iron chains dangle from grandfather's neck? He gave up wearing those iron chains quite a few years ago, at the behest of the new khadim at the dargahsharif (shrine of a Muslim mystic.) For that matter, how is there a black turban on his head? But if Kulsum is, indeed, dreaming how can she hear the shopkeeper say, 'Hey Baikuntha, you are here listening to songs? Let Shaha come, he'll give you a piece of his mind?', loud and clear.* (My translation.)

This encounter between Kulsum and a psychotic Tamijer Baap is an instance of the past-ised subalternity of the historical present—or the past in its subalternity within the historical present—encountering itself as past without presence. That is, it is an encounter between past, as the subalternised discursive appearance of and within the historical present, with itself when it was a present in its emerging, and thus an evental insurgency. This singularising encounter is staged in the novel to depict how that encounter is a command that tends to induce the historical present—as both a dominating identity and a dualising horizon with its metaphysics of presence—to become an open, and thus non-identitarian and singular, present. One that, therefore, will neither itself lapse into nor produce the identity of past. Such a simultaneity of encounter with, living of, command for, and transfiguration into the singular time of open present is constitutive of Benjamin's (2003, p. 395) "now-time" of revolution in its allegoricality-becoming-actuality. There is no doubt that the insurrectionary, or revolutionary, actuality can only be allegorical. But precisely because allegory is a command-giving concept—which arises precisely due to and through the punctuation of the actual—for reconstituting or re-commencing the truncated actuality, it stands validated as such only when allegory is itself sought to be practically actualised by overcoming the historical-discursive confines that instantiate its experiential cognition by being the demonstration of the limit of such experiential cognition. Clearly, allegory and practical actuality of revolution are dialectically bound to each other, and one cannot be itself without the other.

Therefore, the "now-time" of revolution, seen from the vantage point of a historically identified present that is enclosed within the continuum of history, is a spectral temporality. Such a temporality is the space-time constitutive of how things are, for instance, in dream or when one is under the influence of hallucinogens. The dimensions of such a time are inhuman and monstrous. The spectral and ghost-figures that populate Elias's literature, together with the eerie world they compose, are meant precisely to represent such non-human dimensions of space-time in his literature. For, it is through such representation that the affectivity and experience of living such savage and monstrous dimensions of a space and time animated, as it were, by an insurrectionary mind, can be communicated to be induced.

Clearly, the allegorical mode of theorising is continuing the insurrectionary unfolding of life, when that has stalled at the level of practical living, in the register of discourse, and thereby be a lived command—a Dionysian didacticism of desire, so to speak—for the reconstitution and resumption of the insurrection in the empirical practicality of existential living. It would not be an exaggeration to say that such reclamation of the insurrection involves the radicalisation and transfiguration of that empiricality of historically determinate existential living. Elias wants art to perform that allegorical function with regard to stalled unfolding of insurrection. For him that is the only way art can become meaningful. He (2000, p. 5) writes:

"Bengali culture and artistic practice today has been transformed into a monotonous and lifeless habit because of its alienation from the large majority of lower-class Bengalis....

> *What is drummed about as Bengali culture, if that fails to take inspiration from the lives and livelihoods of the majority of the country's people then it too is bound to become as outlandish and groundless as that which is called degenerate culture.* (My translation.)

Elias's creative prose, in its fidelity to its constitutive allegorical modality of thinking and discoursing, performs precisely that gay-scientific function of Dionysian didacticism. What such kind of didacticism amounts to is best explicated by Adorno's (1997, pp. 321-322) reflections on Brecht when the philosopher, while critically engaging with the politico-aesthetic positions of the poet-dramatist, sees the role of the latter's theory inside his creative works. Elias' literary discourse, especially his two novels, end as open texts that give commands precisely through that fact of being open. And their command is to practically live the singularity those texts have grasped and posed in and through the discursive specifications of the determinate existential finitude of their represented world by going beyond it. That is, have the discursive world they represent—or textually constitute—brush against its own constitutive or formational singular grain.

In *Khowabnama*, for instance, the fabulistic-spectral figure of Tamij, which climbs into the moon with its bullet-riddled neck after the life of existentially-lived, sociologically-specified and historically-limited character of Tamij has been ended by the paramilitary shooters, is nothing but an allegory. It is, therefore, a figure whose existence is a command to reclaim it as the singular and singularising constitutivity of Tebhaga in its moment of eruption by continuing to live it beyond its discursively-specified historical and existential finitude. And that, its appearance is meant to allegorically indicate, is achievable only by having that humanly, and thus historically, finite moment stretch itself to its savage, inhuman, monstrous beyond.[6]

NOTES

1. Politics, if one were to speak in the abstract, is against drawing up of boundaries of the perceptible, so it is singularity that in challenging certain historically-given boundaries of the

perceptible, and posing other boundaries for that is how singularity can actualise itself through the mediation of the specificity of a historical situation, redraw boundaries of the perceptible and yield political situations. Thus the political is never singular, it is instead the historically specific situation that mediates the singularity of politics into actuality even while, in the same movement, limiting it.

2. To read Levi-Strauss's conception of the "savage mind", as a principle of the interminable process of dialectical reason, through the prism of Badiou's (2009, p. 189) "a materialism centred upon a theory of the subject" would take that conception to its radical conclusion by setting it free from its original conceptual matrix of structuralism. Such a reading, arguably, renders the conception of the process of dialectical reason—which in Levi-Strauss is a linear, punctuated and bounded interminability—uninterrupted in its interminability, and thus non-linear and unbounded. The two citations below from Badiou (2009, p. 186, p. 189) indicate how inflecting Levi-Strauss's "savage mind" with Badiou's conception of "subjective materiality" would radicalise the former:

   "Materialism stands in internal division to its targets. It is not inexact to see in it a pile of polemical scorn. Its internal makeup is never pacified. Materialism most often *disgusts* the subtle mind.

   "The history of materialism finds the principle of its periodization in its adversary. Making a system out of nothing else than what it seeks to bring down and destroy, puffed up in latent fits of rage, this aim is barely philosophical. It gives colour, in often barbarous inflections, to the impatience of destruction....

   "However, this time of offensive subjectivization produces no stability. We see this as early as in the French Revolution, when the anti-Christian excess of the provisory allies, the plebeians of the cities, is broken by Hebert's execution on the guillotine, whereas the regeneration of spiritualism of the great idealist systems connotes the possibility of a universal concordat. Bourgeois secularism, established through the State, will sometimes be anticlerical, never materialist."

   "Neither God nor Man, in modern idealism, has the function of the organizer of being. The constituent function of language, which excentres every subject-effect, deactivates the materialist operator of the inversion—of the inversion in the sense in which

Marx spoke of putting Hegel back on his feet.

"To claim, by a 'materialist' inversion, to go from the real to the subject means to fall short of modern dialectical criticism, which separates the two terms—subject and real—so that a third, the symbolic or discourse, comes in to operate as a nodal point without for this reason becoming a centre.

"Barred from the path of a simple inversion and summoned to hold onto the scission in which the subject of idealinguistery comes into being as an effect of the chain, we Marxists find ourselves on the dire road of a procedure of destruction-recomposition.

"To pierce through the adversary's line of defence requires this heavy ramrod whose idolatrized head bears our subjective emblems.

"That a conceptual black sheep—a materialism centred upon a theory of the subject—is equally necessary for our most pressing political needs...no doubt proves something...."

3. Subtraction is a concept of politics that comes from Badiou. It is not constitutive of a political move or struggle against power and domination in order to withdraw from or disengage with them. In that, Badiou's concept of subtraction is quite unlike the conception of withdrawal in Martin Heidegger that is concomitant with his concept of "ontological difference". Rather, subtraction is constitutive of the political manoeuvre—or struggle—to break with the horizon constitutive of domination and competition and its dualised and dualising structure, in the process unravelling and destroying it. "Ontological subtraction", pace Badiou, is a conceptual figure of singularity that is the science of revolutionary politics, or praxis as ontology.
4. The conception of allegory as command—which is premised here on the asymmetrical dialectic, and thus torsion, between the particularity of the sensuous and affective ("beauty", "material", "individual") on one hand, and the generality of the cognitive ("divine", "transcendental", "moral", "ethical) on the other – is derived from a reading of Walter Benjamin's 'Allegory and Trauerspiel', the last chapter of his *The Origin of German Tragic Drama*. It is precisely this asymmetrical dialectic, and the concomitant torsion, that Benjamin reveals to be the defining characteristic of the Baroque allegory when he (2003, p. 160)

affirmatively explicates the Baroque allegorical principle through his criticism of the classicist, as also the romantic, "symbol" for effacing this dialectical asymmetry between those aspects in order to present them as an organic harmony: "The unity of the material and the transcendental object, which constitutes the paradox of the theological symbol, is distorted into a relationship between appearance and essence. The introduction of this distorted conception of the symbol into aesthetics was a romantic and destructive extravagance which preceded the desolation of modern art criticism. As a symbolic construct, the beautiful is supposed to merge with the divine in an unbroken whole. The idea of the unlimited immanence of the moral world in the world of beauty is derived from the theosophical aesthetics of the romantics. But the foundations of this idea were laid long before. In classicism the tendency to the apotheosis of existence in the individual who is perfect, in more than an ethical sense, is clear enough.... But once the ethical subject has become absorbed in the individual, then no rigorism—not even Kantian rigorism—can save it and preserve its masculine profile. Its heart is lost in the beautiful soul. And the radius of action—no, only the radius of the culture—of the thus perfected beautiful individual is what describes the circle of the 'symbolic'. In contrast the baroque apotheosis is a dialectical one. It is accomplished in the movement between extremes."

It must also be stated here as an aside that the principle of baroque allegory bears, in Benjamin's affirmative exposition of it, a strong conceptual affinity with the conception of philosophy of history that comes from Marx. The latter (dialectical materialism) is, clearly, not an epistemology of history as a presence-at-hand or identitarian existence. Hence, it is also not a code of moral, or conventional, directive to live (or live in) that empirical history as such. Rather, it is a philosophy of the moment of formation or making of history that is logically prior to the moment of history as such. Clearly, the Marxian philosophy of history—or dialectical materialism—is a philosophy that seeks its own realisation in and as the practicality of politics precisely by abolishing itself as the discursivised concept it is. It is "philosophy" only when it is, to cite Badiou's Althusserian maxim, "under the condition of politics". Such a philosophy of (more accurately, for) the making of history is, to resort to Benjamin once again, history brushed against its own grain.

5. "Present without presence" is present as and in its own presencing, and is thus precisely difference (differing away) from presence. Hence, "present without presence" does not pose itself in a manner so as to have its existential affirmation as itself produce an identified past of itself. "Present without presence" is present that does not become past and thus has no past. It is not present as a historical identity, something which as that historical identity produces its constitutively contradictory identity of past (which is basically the present that has become absent as the presence it was).
6. There is this one other aspect of Elias that has not been dealt with here directly. Albeit, it has been adequately prefigured by what has been argued here. Nevertheless, that aspect should at least be briefly stated. It is to do with Elias's postcoloniality. The contention being that Elias is thoroughly immersed in his postcolonial historical situation and is yet a producer of a literary and theoretical discourse that is, by no stretch of imagination or argument, postcolonialist. The former is on account of his intellectual organicity while the latter is due to his political Jacobinism. We could well call him a seasoned Leninist for not conflating and confounding concrete situation with concrete analysis—or the historical with historicity—and for rigorously grasping them in terms of dialectical asymmetry. This aspect of Elias is, arguably, best revealed through an analysis of the influence of the Bangla novelist and short-story writer Manik Bandopadhyay's prose on Elias fiction and the latter's own active engagement with Bandopadhyay, particularly in his essay, *Manik Bandopadhyayer Ragi Chokher Sapna* (The Dream of Manik Bandopadhyay's Angry Eyes), in his *Sanskritir Bhanga Setu* (The Broken Bridge of Culture).

REFERENCES

Adorno, Theodor W., *Aesthetic Theory*, tr. Robert Hullot-Kentor, eds. Gretel Adorno and Rolf Tiedmann (Continuum, London, 1997).

Badiou, Alain, 'The Indissoluble Salt of Truth'. In *Theory of the Subject*, tr. Bruno Bosteels (Continuum, London, 2009).

Badiou, Alain, 'The Black Sheep of Materialism'. In *Theory of the Subject*, tr. Bruno Bosteels (Continuum, London, 2009).

Badiou, Alain, 'One, Multiple, Multiplicities'. In *Theoretical Writings*, edited and translated by Ray Brassier and Alberto Toscano (Continuum, London, 2010).

Balibar, Etienne, 'The Elements of the Structure and their History'. In *Reading Capital* by Louis Althusser and Etienne Balibar, tr. Ben Brewster (Verso, London, 1999).

Benjamin, Walter, 'Allegory and Trauerspiel'. In *The Origin of German Tragic Drama*, tr. John Osborne (Verso, London, 1998).

Benjamin, Walter, 'On the Concept of History'. In *Selected Writings* (Volume 4), tr. Edmund Jephcott and Others, eds. Marcus Bullock, Howard Eiland and Michael W. Jennings (The Belknap Press of Harvard University Press, Cambridge, Massachusetts, 2006).

Derrida, Jacques, *Spectres of Marx*, tr. Peggy Kamuf (Routledge, London, 1994).

Elias, Akhtaruzzaman, *Chilekotar Sepai* [Soldier in the Attic] (The University Press Limited, Dhaka, 2000).

Elias, Akhtaruzzaman, *Khowabnama* [Dream Chronicle] (Naya Udyog, Kolkata, 1998).

Elias, Akhtaruzzaman, *Galpa Samagra* [Collected Stories] (Naya Udyog, Kolkata, 2000).

Elias, Akhtaruzzaman, *Sanskritir Bhanga Setu* [The Broken Bridge of Culture: Essays on Literature, Society and Culture] (Naya Udyog, Kolkata, 2000).

Gramsci, Antonio, 'Problems of Marxism'. In *Selections from the Prison Notebooks* edited and translated by Quintin Hoare and Geoffrey Nowell Smith (Orient Longman, Hyderabad, 1996).

Levi-Strauss, Claude, 'History and Dialectic'. In *The Savage Mind*, (The University of Chicago Press, 1966).

Marx, Karl, 'The Trinity Formula'. In *Capital*, Volume III, ed. Frederick Engels (Progress Publishers, Moscow, 1986).

Ranciere, Jacques, 'The Politics of Literature'. In *The Politics of Literature*, tr. Julie Rose (Polity, Cambridge, 2011).

Williams, Raymond, 'Structures of Feeling'. In *Marxism and Literature* (Oxford University Press, Oxford, 2010).

Literature in Use: The Muktibodh Alibi

Literature and Politics: Singularity Against Sovereignty

Can ambition stand on the shoulders of modesty? In this essay I intend to court failure in seeking to make that impossibility happen. I have, to begin with, set myself the rather unremarkable task of sharing with you an intimately subjective question that I often grapple with. This question, which presses insistently on my consciousness, especially when I read Muktibodh, has to do with the relationship (if any) between literature and politics. The question stems from the fact of two selves comprising my individuality: one that is compelled to engage, in some measure, with the politics of movements, especially working-class movement; and the other driven by its love for literature. I often wonder about what possible connection there might be between the two. My militant concern leads me to think that proletarian culture, in the final analysis, is the revolutionary movement of the working class as its own expression or form. In that context, do art and literature make any sense whatsoever for the working-class movement and its culture? Can I then justifiably speak of a relationship between literature and politics just because they happen to inhabit me as two indispensable alterities of my individual self? Or, is it that they coexist, side by side but separately, within the same individual, and thus in no apparent relation with each other? I would wish to cautiously suggest that it is the latter. But then considering that the two exist within the same individual self in a kind of separateness, such separated coexistence must be accounted for. In other words, what exactly is the meaning this separated, this non-relational coexistence—of love for literature and the compulsion to be engaged with radical political movements—imply? My contention here would be that politics is precisely what is at stake in the meaning implied by such separateness.

Clearly, I am here trying not merely to share my personal anxieties with you as I said I would. Instead, I am, in the process of laying bare those anxieties and the neurotic restlessness they comprise, loosely organising them as concepts into what can provisionally be called a militant protocol of reading literature. And Muktibodh, inasmuch as his work is arguably constitutive of such a question about the relationship (or not) between literature and politics, and its attendant anxieties and struggles, is, in my view, a perfect alibi for that. However, since he is only an alibi, the reading of his work here will neither be textually exhaustive nor canonically organised. Instead, my reading of Muktibodh will be capriciously subjective, and thus arbitrary, scattered, desultory and thin.

Before I cherry-pick a few things from Muktibodh's complex and highly ramified oeuvre to explicate the meaning and significance of separated coexistence (or compossibility) of literature and movemental politics, we would do well to make sense of this non-relational coexistence in terms of literature and its use. What exactly is at stake when one talks about the usefulness of literature? More pertinently, what does *use* mean when we talk about the use of literature?

Jameson (2000, p. 2) offers a few clues when he writes: "Brecht would have been delighted, I like to think, at an argument, not for his greatness, or his canonicity, nor even for some new and unexpected value of posterity (let alone for his 'postmodernity'), as rather for his *usefulness*...." Further on he clarifies what he means by *use* in the context of Brecht and his literary work: "'Usefulness' in this context would not only mean 'didactic'.... Yet if it means didactic, then we must add that Brecht never exactly had a doctrine to teach, not even 'Marxism' in the form of a system ('The ABC of...,' to recall a once-fashionable way of doing it): rather, we will want to show... that his 'proposals' and his lessons—the fables and the proverbs he delighted in offering—were more on the order of a method than a collection of facts, thoughts, convictions, first principles, and the like. Yet it was an equally sly 'method', which equally successfully eludes all the objections modern philosophy (as in Gadamer's *Truth and Method*) has persuasively made against the reifications of the methodological as such." [Emphasis author's.]

This indicates how usefulness must be grasped not in terms of reified instrumentalism but in terms of what Marx conceptualised as "use-value"; the radical inverse of such instrumentalism. Usefulness or use, in this Marxian sense of use-value, lies in it being for itself. More accurately, something as use-value means it is its own 'measure'. That is to say, the usefulness of any activity, and its end, can be grasped only in terms of its performance being immeasurable against something else. To measure it thus—which would give it a value either greater or less than that with regard to which it is being measured—transforms it into exchange-value. Then the value of an activity is determined not for being what it is in and for itself—that is, as use-value—but rather what it is vis-à-vis something else. This would amount to the repression of its *usefulness* because use-value is precisely that which is not captured by any such measure, and the relationality such measure entails. Marx (1986, p. 45) clearly indicates this antagonism between use-value and exchange-value when he lays bare the internally-divided character of commodity: "As use-values, commodities are, above all, of different qualities but as exchange-values they are merely different quantities, and consequently do not contain an atom of use-value."

What this arguably demonstrates, therefore, is that exchange-value inevitably amounts to instrumentalism, and the concomitant repression of usefulness. For, when something is grasped in terms of its exchange-value it is grasped not in terms of what it is, or can be, an accomplishment of by virtue of the material properties that comprise it in its singularity, but in terms of how it is exchanged with other things. Therefore, to the extent that use-value is an activity for its own end, it stands for the collapse of the means/ends duality, or, in Marx's (1986, p. 55) language of critique of political economy, the collapse of the mutually hierarchised and thus accidental but competitive duality of "relative value-form" and "equivalent value-form". Hence, usefulness, in this sense of use-value, if thought in terms of its generalisability, is a break with, and collapse of, the exchange-principle and the structure of relationality this principle is constitutive of. Use, or use-value, is non-exchange and non-relational and is, thus, irreplaceable or singular.

In that context, to envisage the use of art and literature vis-à-vis radical movemental politics in terms of how the former can be the latter's instrument is to lapse into the regime of exchange, and its constitutive law of value, in the very moment that such a regime is sought to be challenged, broken with and decimated. Therefore, we would do well, instead, to think and envisage the question of usefulness of art in terms of art as its own end. Before this is mistaken for some kind of an aestheticist proposal of art for art's sake, I must immediately insist that it is meant to be quite the contrary. It is, arguably, an attempt to resignify art for art's sake as a proposal for revolutionary politics. For, insofar as revolutionary politics seeks to break with and decimate the structure of exchange and relationality, this is the only pertinent way to think the use of art and literature from its vantage-point.

It must be clarified here that this proposal to think and envisage literature as its own end is not—unlike the art-for-art's-sake formulation of the aestheticists—an affirmation of literature as a sovereign identity. It is, instead, meant to be an affirmation of the eventality, or generic subtraction (Badiou, 2007) from the structure of exchange, relationality and identity that literature *is* in its emerging. Therefore, art (literature in our case) as its own end is, in this instance, not an aestheticist proposal for the autonomy of art. Instead, it is a blow for the "autonomy of the aesthetic process" (Badiou, 2013). I hope to demonstrate soon that Muktibodh's literature induces its readers to read it specifically in those terms and generally adopt such an approach to the twin-questions of politics of literature, and literature and politics. But before that we need to figure how our argument for the autonomy of the aesthetic process is radically antagonistic to the aestheticist proposal for the sovereignty (read identitarian autonomy) of art (or literature).

The aestheticist affirmation of the sovereignty of art or literature is an affirmation of the autonomy of art or literature as an identity. An affirmation that restores the very structure of exchange and relationality that art or literature in its emerging is a generic and determinate subtraction from. Therefore, the aesthetic process, which is what is actualised in art in its moment of emerging, is the subtraction that our proposal of art as its own end affirms. But to the extent that this autonomising process is interrupted by the identity of art in whose moment of emerging lies its actuality, the autonomy of art as its performative, or gestic, process of subtraction is radically separate from and antagonistic to the sovereignty (read identitarian autonomy) of art.

The question before us is, therefore, how to affirm literature as its own end in the sense of it being a generic incarnation of the process of subtraction from the structure of exchange and relationality, and thereby, in the same movement, disavow literature as a sovereign identity? If art, or literature, emerges vis-à-vis non-art or non-literature, it must be grasped in that emerging as determinate subtraction from the relational structure of determination and negation that is specified in and through determination by the latter. This means that art in its emerging negates the absence of art. In other words, art in its emerging must negate the determining presence of non-art, whose existence as such testifies to the absence of art and can, therefore, be seen as the prevention of the emerging of art. And in so negating non-art, art in its emerging must simultaneously and prefiguratively negate itself as the determination it is itself bound to lapse into on account of that first negation. Otherwise, art would inevitably become an identity and concomitantly restore the structure of exchange and relationality, and its constitutive logic of determination that it tended to disavow in order to emerge. As a result, art in its identitarianised moment would be drawn into the structural web of competing determinations—perpetual alternation of determination and negation—and thus be compelled and constrained by the sheer objective fact of its identitarianised existence to either determine or be determined, to instrumentalise or be instrumentalised. Clearly then, it would cease to be the use-value, an activity for its own end, that it incarnated in its moment of pre-identitarian emerging. To grasp art thus, is to grasp it in its evanescent subtractiveness from the structure of exchange, relationality and instrumentalism. In other words, art is discerned as subtraction only when it is grasped in terms of it implying its own negation as a *thing* or an identity in terms of its moment of emerging in order to sustain that process of emerging beyond itself. Only then can we claim to have grasped and envisaged art as use-value or art as its own end. Thus affirmation of literature as its own end, insofar as it in its emerging is the actuality of the process of determinate subtraction, is truly such an affirmation only when literature is seen either to be positing (from the side of the reader) or made to pose and envisage (from the side of the author) the simultaneous negation of itself as an identity and/or determination.

Muktibodh's Difficult Commitment: Art As (Re-) Commencement of Politics

In this light, let us now turn to Muktibodh by focusing our attention on the opening shot of Mani Kaul's *Satah se Uthata Aadmi* (Man Arising From the Surface), a film on the poet's life and letters. The scene is that of a fragment of a North Indian small-town landscape—with dawn breaking over it—seen from inside a house through its rear window that suddenly clams shut on it. This shot or image must arguably be seen as a metaphor of Muktibodh's politico-aesthetic vision as affirmed in his literature. It is, as far as metaphors go, quite accurate and apposite. It reveals Muktibodh's vision, as envisaged in his literature, of how art begins (must begin!) with the interruption of politics.

To put this in another way, the birth of art is the recommencement, at the level of the individual, of that which movemental politics incarnates at the social level of abstraction. For Muktibodh, art is, as the opening shot of Kaul's film metaphorically reveals, all about how the individual resumes, must resume, in his 'interiority' that which he sees as being interrupted in the world outside. A move that would amount to constellating the 'interiority' of the individual with the exteriority of society to yield a new order of sociality. One that is constitutive of the abolition of the stratified identitarian dichotomy of interiority (individual) and exteriority (society) in order to preserve them as simultaneous moments of difference-as-its-own-deployment constitutive of one single perpetual process of uninterrupted dispersion. Muktibodh's literature is a testament to the fact that this is how he experienced his own literary-creative process as a poet, who was also an engaged communist militant. In his essay, *Teesra Kshan* (The Third Moment), Muktibodh (2002, p. 13) shows himself telling his friend and literary alter-ego Keshav:

> *Hindi mey mann se baahe vastu ko hi vastu samjha jata hai—aisa mera khayal hai. Main kehta hoon ki mann ka tatva bhi vastu ho sakta hai. Aur agar yeh maaan liya jaye ki mann ka tatva bhi ek vastu hai to aise tatva ke saath tadaakaarita ya taadaatmya ka koi matlab nahin hota kyun ki weh tatva mann ka hi ek bhag hai. Haan, main is mann ke tatva ke saath tatasthata ke rukh ki kalpna kar sakta hoon; tadaakarita ka nahin.*

(In Hindi, only that which lies outside the mind is considered an object—that is my belief. I say the substance of the mind can also be an object. And if we are to accept that the substance of the mind is also an object, then there is really no sense of oneness or identity with such a substance because that substance is part of the mind. Yes, I can imagine an attitude of detachment towards this substance of the mind, not of oneness.) [My translation.] Later on in the same essay, he has Keshav tell him (2002, p. 18): *Kewal tatastha vyakti hi tadaakar ho sakta hai, samjhe?* (Only a detached person can be in a state of oneness, understood?) [My translation.]

What Muktibodh attempts to reveal through this dialogic scene he sets up between him and his friend is that oneness/ unity (*tadaakarita*) is not about reconciliation of mutually dualised and identitarianised terms (of *mann* and *baahe vastu*) into a system constitutive of contradictions—exactly that which affirmative negation *is* in Hegel's philosophy of idealistic and symmetrical dialectic, and in capitalism too. Instead, unity, for him, is the uninterrupted continuity of the process of *deployment of difference*, incarnated in and as a specific difference in its emerging, as disavowal of identity. What we have here, therefore, are two radically separate and antagonistic temporalities, historicities or epochalities of unity: conjunctural and constellational. The second, which is what Muktibodh upholds, is difference as its own process of deployment in its own time of being uninterrupted. While the first, which is through and through Hegelian, is history as the linear time of totalisation of different space-times of social existence into a stratified hierarchy of identities, or lapsed difference. The first temporality, precisely because it does not reflexively grasp its own conjunctural, overdetermined nature, continues as such. The second, on the other hand, emerges from within the first overdetermined epochality as a break with it through and as an embodiment of the reflexive awareness of the overdetermined, conjunctural nature of the first temporality. Pace Althusser, this is how one ought to distinguish between the Hegelian and the Marxian conceptions of social and historical reality.

Now, difference tends to turn into identity due to the lapse of the process of deployment of difference it is an evanescent incarnation of. In such circumstances, one can affirm unity as continuity of the process of deployment of difference only through a detached disposition towards that which is yielded as identity in it having been the determinate, and thus evanescent, actuality of difference-in-its-own-deployment. Clearly, only through detachment from identity, yielded by the lapse of the process of difference as its own deployment, can one reclaim that process, and affirm it.

Thus, the process of difference-as-its-own-deployment can be one with itself—or a unity unto itself—only in its uninterrupted continuity. And in order for it to be uninterruptedly continuous, the various constitutive moments of that process must prefigure the overcoming of determinations or identities they themselves would respectively tend to lapse into. That, needless to say, requires a capacity for detachment (*tatasthata*) towards such identities in order to be able to leave them behind through their critical overcoming. That would ensure that every determinate moment of the process of difference as its own deployment—incarnated by those identities in their respective moments of pre-identitarian emerging—is one (*tadaakar*) with every other such moment in and as the uninterrupted process of difference-as-its-own-deployment. The Muktibodh essay in question is an explication of this asymmetrical (and thus materialist) dialectic of faith and detachment, and detachment as faith, and the "difficult commitment" of subtraction this particular dialectical approach is integral to. Badiou (2003, pp. 63-64) would doubtless call this Muktibodh's "fidelity to the event".

Continuous Production and Universal Singularity: Truth-Procedurality of Art

Now since we know that art in its moment of emerging tends to recommence, albeit at a different level of abstraction, that which has lapsed in the interruption of movemental politics, we also ought to understand that such recommencement constitutes itself through and as disavowal of the determination the interruption in question amounts to. Two things ought to become perfectly clear from this. One, the determination or identity this interruption of movemental politics yields is historical or societal vis-à-vis the subject-position of the individual. Something that, therefore, renders the latter a determinate ground and thus also a generic condition to re-think and/or re-incarnate subtraction from the structure of exchange and relationality specified by the identity and determination of the historical or societal. Two, interruption of movemental politics is nothing other than the interruption of a determinate subtraction, precisely due to its ineluctable ontological condition of being determinate.

Hence, interruption of a determinate subtraction can, and must, be prospectively seen as the moment of lapse of what would otherwise be the uninterrupted simultaneity of different determinate subtractions in their infinity. For, as we have noted earlier, art grasps and thus poses itself as the subtraction it determinately is in its emerging only if it simultaneously anticipates the overcoming of itself as the identity it will tend to lapse into on account of its determinate subtractive emerging. This uninterrupted simultaneity of infinitely different determinate subtractions would be the simultaneity of "infinite difference and infinite deployment of infinite difference". (Badiou, 2005, pp. ix-x.) That would, therefore, be nothing but the process by which "generic singularities partake" of one another. (Badiou, 2005, p. 76.). Therefore, not only is the process of generic singularities partaking of each other generic, but, for Badiou, the processes constitutive of this process are also generic. The process of subtraction becoming itself in order to be, which Badiou alternately calls "subtractive ontology" (2005, p. 17) or "universal singularity" (2003, pp. 14-15), is the ceaseless process constitutive of this uninterrupted simultaneity of infinite difference and infinite deployment of infinite difference. Clearly, therefore, mutual partaking of generic singularities—which could well be called the intersubjectivity of encounter, as opposed to the capitalist intersubjectivity of exchange—amounts to continuous production a la Brecht.[1] This Brechtian continuous production obviates distributive transformation of alterities (actually, generic singularities of differences-as-their-own-deployment) into stratified identities (or particularities) and is, therefore, the preclusion and abolition of social division of labour or class relations.

Brechtian continuous production amounts to every moment of production simultaneously tending to be a moment of consumption and vice-versa. It is, therefore, clearly constitutive of the abolition and preclusion of both the producer/consumer (or writer/reader) duality and split, and the relational structure of competing determinations or the endless alternation between negation and determination that such duality and split are constitutive of. This also means that continuous production as abolition and preclusion of social division of labour is production as pure expenditure and is hence constitutive of the radical inverse of capitalism as a restricted economy of accumulation. It is tantamount to an economy of discharge, which in Bataille's (1998, pp. 21-23) words is "the general economy" of expenditure. Clearly, Brecht's continuous production is a move into production of politics from the capitalist, class-divided horizon of politics of production. And it consists in the intersubjectivity of encounter founding itself as its own "subjective materiality" (Badiou, 2009, p. 198) of what can be termed relationality of the nonrelational.[2]

Therefore, to the extent that the limiting of subtraction due to its determinate condition is, to speak prospectively or in the future-anterior, the lapse of the uninterrupted simultaneity of different determinate subtractions in their infinity, it amounts to the interruption of Brechtian continuous production. And art, as we have seen earlier, is characterised as the generic condition for re-thinking subtractive ontology, or Brecht's continuous production, on account of it in its emerging having determinately incarnated subtraction at the individual level of abstraction. It is the specificity of this determinate level of the individual that defines the subtractive emerging at that level in its characteristic genericness as art. It is for this reason that art is a generic subtraction or singularity and, therefore, a generic procedure for the universalisability of the truth of the singular it was in its determinately subtractive emerging (event). It would, therefore, make sense to state here in passing that Badiou's (2005, pp. 124-126) concept of "truth-procedure" is arguably cognate with Benjamin's concept of allegory.

The truth-procedurality of art is generic in two senses. First, it is what Badiou clearly intends it to be: a procedure for the universalisability of the truth of the singular—which as its universality would be mutual partaking of singularities or Brechtian continuous production—in the internality of the field of art itself. Second, it is a procedure that in and through its determinateness and aesthetic paradigmaticness poses the universalisability of the truth of determinate subtraction as various generic singularities (including art itself) partaking of one another. This is arguably our interpretative expansion of the scope and remit of the concept of generic truth-procedure, albeit one that is logically consistent with and clearly implied by its place in Badiou's philosophical discourse. That would, it must be reiterated here yet again, amount to generic singularities, among them art and politics, prefiguring in their determinate emerging the overcoming of the identities they would tend to lapse into. What this in its infinitely open entirety would yield is subtractive ontology as the interminable and uninterrupted process of becoming-subtraction.

Subtraction, were we to grasp it in its determinateness at the individual level of abstraction, is emancipation of desire because it in its emerging is a disavowal of determination. In such a situation, the generic truth-procedure of art actualised in the internality of its own paradigmatic domain as multiple generic singularities of determinate eruptions or events of works, forms, genres and media of art, would amount to Brechtian continuous production on and through those multiple determinate planes constitutive of the paradigmatic domain of art. That would mean the interminable mutation of works, forms, genres and media of art both within and among themselves.

As a result, the individual level of abstraction would be rendered a terrain of radical antagonism between the temporality of constellation and uninterrupted dispersion, and the temporality of consolidation of deep selfhood through distributive transformation of alterities into a systemic self of stratified identities.

And what is desire at the individual level of abstraction are productive forces at the scale and level of abstraction of the social. Hence, subtraction at the level of the social is nothing but the unshackling of productive forces from the shackles of social relations of production. Thus we may well broadly say that the social has two levels of abstraction: one that is known by its own name of the social while the other is that of the individual. And while the first is the plane of contention against the determination of history/society, the second is a plane of struggle to disavow and overcome the determination of psychology.

Psychologisation of the individual is transformation of the subject-position or level of abstraction of the individual into a gathered, consolidated self. It is, to be more precise, the distributive transformation of alterities at the individual level of abstraction into a totalised and totalising system of stratified sub-selves. The gathered or coherent individual self is this totalised and totalising system or temporality. Similarly, historicalisation of the social consists in transformation of the subject-position or level of abstraction of the social into a gathered, consolidated society through the distributive stratification of different space-times of social existence into a class-divided and totalising temporality. In other words, psychology is the concept of the totalising and total structure of exchange and relationality as incarnated by and at the individual level of abstraction. On the other hand, the same structural logic in being incarnated at the post-individual, social level of abstraction becomes history.

Hence, art and politics as generic procedures for universalisability of the truth of singularity (or determinate subtraction) demonstrate that revolutionary transformation is necessarily a Freudo-Marxist problematic. It must be noted here that the truth of the singular (event) or determinate subtraction in its universalised actuality would be mutual partaking of generic singularities, or Brechtian continuous production. A note of caution must, however, be sounded here. The affirmation of Freudo-Marxism as the science of revolutionary transformation is by no means a call for an eclectic combination of two disparate doctrines. Rather, what is at stake here is their synthesis that derives from the experiential understanding that the project of Freudian psychoanalysis in constituting and affirming the individual's disavowal of his objectification (actually subjectivation) by psychology continues the Marxist project which demonstrates that the social is not meant to be the object of history. This clearly shows that both need each other to complement and complete themselves.

Desire, Idea, Poetry: A Case for Freudo-Marxism

I hope that as we go along we will be able to grasp Muktibodh's literature as an affirmation of, among other things, such Freudo-Marxism. For now, let us keep in mind the last four significantly indicative lines of his (1988, p. 11) poem, *Poonjiwadi Samaj ke Prati* (To the Capitalist Society), that can arguably be seen as a credo of the politico-aesthetic vision of Freudo-Marxism: revolution as an uninterrupted continuity of the unleashing of desire/productive forces in, through and beyond the individual and social levels of abstraction, and the concomitant destruction of capital as the structure of exchange. That, in other words, would be the generic singularities of art and politics partaking of one another.

Meri jwaal, jan ki jwaal hokar ek
Aapni ushnata se dho chalen avivek
Tu hai maran, tu hai rikt, tu hai vyarth
tera dhwans keval ek tera aarth.

("My fire, and the fire of the masses become one/To wash the irrational with our heat/You are death, you are emptiness, you are useless/Your only meaning is your destruction.") [My translation.]

Here it might be productive to take into account one of Badiou's key proposals on theatre. He writes in his 'Rhapsody for the Theatre: A Short Philosophical Treatise': "We can...be sure that philosophy and psychoanalysis recognize that the operations of the theatre take place on their respective terrains, and thus *at the intersection, which is always in dispute, of these territories.*" (Emphasis author's). He then develops this argument of his to conclude: "Theatre: the putting-into-bodies of the Idea. From the point of desire, it is its life; from the point of the Idea, it is its tomb.... Theatre as bastard philosophy, or philosophical bastardy: principled impurity, diverted lesson, all-too-serious analysis, all-too-ludic truth to be assured. A revolving door." As long as we remember to grasp and envisage all art, literature included, for the subtractive performativity it primarily is, this Badiouian formulation on theatre could, perhaps at the risk of some oversimplification, be applied to art in general.

Art is psychoanalytical insofar as it in its emerging is unleashing of desire from its censorship and thus distortion by a deep psychological self at the individual level of abstraction. Therefore, it is, in its lapsed state, an Idea of the truth of subtraction, and thus a procedure for the recommencement of the truth of the singular (or determinate subtraction) and its universalisability: the interminable and uninterrupted process of becoming-subtraction. But given that art is a generic truth-procedure for the recommencement and universalisability of the truth of the subtractive, such recommencement that it ideationally is, and thus procedurally articulates, is as much for its own individual level of abstraction in its paradigmatic internality as for the social level of abstraction that its lapse into an identitarianised individual self reconstitutes as an incarnation of both psychology with regard to its own internality as a level of abstraction, and history with regard to the social level of determination that the individual self in being that identity is constitutive of as its definitional, identitarianising and relational point of reference. Politics would be the determinate and generic recommencement of subtraction at the social level of abstraction in and as disavowal of the determination of history. As the generic recommencement or re-actualisation of the Idea of subtraction as its own truth at the determinate level of the social, it would be unshackling of productive forces from the social relations of production constitutive of history. And considering that politics would be the actualisation of the unleashing of desire (productive forces) at that determinate level, it too would be a generic subtraction or generic singularity and thus, should, in turn, consequently also be grasped as a generic procedure for the universalisability of the truth of the subtractive or the singular. Such universalisability would be different generic singularities partaking of one another.

However, to the extent that constitutive moments of the process of becoming-subtraction, or Brechtian continuous production, are moments of determinate subtraction, there is always the risk of subtraction being interrupted at those moments because they are its determinate actualities. Thence, art as "principled impurity", "diverted lesson", "all-too-ludic truth to be assured". It is for this reason we would be right in following Badiou to insist that art would be "the putting-into-bodies of the Idea. From the point of desire, it is its life; from the point of the Idea, it is its tomb".

Muktibodh too has a similar conception of the dialectic of desire/affect and idea with regard to literature, particularly poetry. In *Teesra Kshan* (The Third Moment), he (2002, p. 20) has Keshav tell him:

> *Tum mey aur mujhme ek bada bhed hai. Vichar mujhe utteyjit kar ke kriyavaan kar dete hain. Vicharon ko tum turant hi samvednayon mey parinat kar dete ho. Phir unhi samvednayon ke tum chitra banate ho. Vicharon kee parinati samvednayon mey aur samvednayon kee chitron mey. Iss prakaar tum mey ye do parinatiyan hain.*

(There is a big distinction between you and me. Ideas excite me and make me active. You immediately convert ideas into affects.

Then from those affects you make images. Conversion of ideas into affects and affects into images. In this fashion there are these two moments of transformation in you.) [My translation.]

Through Keshav, Muktibodh attempts to tell us what he thinks his poetic practice to be and, in the process, also affirm it. Such a poetic practice, by virtue of being conversion of ideas into affects, and conversion, once again, of those affects into images, demonstrate that for him the idea of the truth can be actual only in, as and through its affective, performative and thus determinate realisation. What is at stake in this conversion of ideas into affects is not the determination of the body, as a materiality of affects, by ideas. Something that Keshav, by his own admission, is prone to as opposed to Muktibodh. Rather, Muktibodh's poetry, not unlike theatre for Badiou, is about ideas in their affective embodiment, "the putting-into-bodies of the Idea". This singular moment of embodiment of the idea is the moment of the collapse of the idea/body duality.

Conversely, therefore, the idea, for Muktibodh a la his alter-ego Keshav, is that which in and through its discursivity communicates itself as the non-discursive truth of affective eruption in its determinate actualisation. That is because the idea as that discursivity is a lapsed incarnation of that affective eruption. Hence, he too seems to be envisaging and explicating poetry as something that operates *"at the intersection...of these* (two) *territories"* of psychoanalysis on one hand, and philosophy under the conditions of art and politics on the other. Like Badiou, the whole point of the idea for Muktibodh is for it to be caught in this dialectical situation of "principled impurity". That, he appears to suggest, is how the Idea retains its productivity in both radical aesthetics and radical politics. Not surprisingly, Badiou's "bastard philosophy" and "philosophical bastardy" echo the dialectical reflexivity of *samvednatmak gyan* (affective knowledge) and *gyanatmak samvedna* (knowledge-informed affect), through which Muktibodh in this essay constellates *bhokta* (one who experiences) and *darshak* (the spectator) thus abolishing and precluding their divided and stratified distribution.

Subsequently, we find Keshav tell Muktibodh (2002, p. 20):

> *Agar tumhari kavitayen kisee ko uljhi huyee maloom hon toh tumhe hataash nahin hona chahhiye...main tumhari kavitayen dhyan se padhta hoon.*

(You shouldn't despair if someone finds yours poems convoluted...I read your poems carefully.) About those poems, he further says:

> *Unmey aur safai kee jaroorat hai. Kintu main un logon ka samarthak nahin hoon jo safai ke naam per, safai ke liye 'content' (kavya-tatva) kee bali de dete hain.*

(They need more clarity. But I am not a supporter of those people who in the name of chiselling a poem, for the sake of its clarity, sacrifice its content.) [My translation.]

This is clearly meant to be an affirmation of a kind of poetry that through a dialectically articulated reflexivity seeks to demonstrate, from the poet's end itself, the subtraction it is an interruption of. And this it does by amply and appropriately indicating its subtractive emerging as the excess of its identitarianised interruption. After all, what would it mean for a poem to sacrifice its content for a clean, well-wrought form? Something that Muktibodh has Keshav criticise and reject. Clearly, this content, which the poem can, through its well-wrought and pat form, completely repress and render invisible, is this excess. So, what Keshav calls content of a poem is not simply meant to be the substance that is held within form as if the latter were a neutral vessel. Rather, it is what formalists such as Viktor Shklovsky conceptually designated as "content of form". This "content of form"—it must be repeated here in order to be free of all ambiguity—is the constitutivity of a form in its subtractive emerging, and hence also its excess.

In this context, let us once again examine the conception of usefulness of art with regard to politics. We must, without doubt, talk about the usefulness of art in terms of the instruction that art gives politics. But this usefulness or didacticism of art vis-à-vis politics is not what the discursive terms or features of a work, form, genre and/or medium of art convey to politics. That would be oh-so-many reifications of the former and its concomitant instrumentalisation by the latter. Rather, the instruction that art offers, or at any rate should offer, is all about art communicating itself in terms of the subtraction and disavowal of determination, and thus the unleashing of desire, it incarnated in its determinate and generic moment of emerging. We may, therefore, term the didacticism of art, which constitutes its usefulness, as didacticism of desire. This is arguably how Brecht sought to grasp and envisage didacticism —particularly with regard to art, but also politics—in and through his theory and practice of dramaturgy and literature.

The Brechtian conception of axiomatics[3] is an articulation of this didacticism of desire, which demonstrates how the revolutionary social is the actuality of the process of (interminable) scission or uninterrupted dispersion. This conception of axiomatics consists of grasping the Idea in its internal division due to the dynamic of desire (or productive forces) being an asymmetrical dialectic of its unshackling (emancipation) and harnessing (interruption/distortion). The "revolving door" of generic singularity (desire and psycho-analysis) and generic truth-procedure (Idea and philosophy) that we see Badiou articulate with regard to theatre is a reformulation of Brechtian axiomatics, and the attendant conception of didacticism of desire and its actualisation as continuous production. This means art instructs the social level of determination by posing the overcoming of its own identitarianisation as art to recommence the subtraction or unleashing of desire that it *was* in its moment of determinate emerging.

Aesthetic education is not, or cannot be, discursive education. It is affective and gestic/performative education. To further clarify what this means, let us cite an oft-quoted and much-celebrated passage from Marx (1984, p. 21): "Just as one does not judge an individual by what he thinks about himself, so one cannot judge...a period of transformation by its consciousness, but, on the contrary, this consciousness must be explained from the contradictions of material life, from the conflict existing between the social forces of production and the relations of production." From such a Marxian vantage-point, art must be judged not by what it says about itself through the discursive features and contours of its various works, forms, genres, and/or media but by explaining why and how those discursive features and contours are organised the way they are as those works, forms, genres, and/or media in question. That is to say, one can judge what art is only by grasping the organisations of its discursive features and contours that its works, forms, genres, media and the like are, in terms of what they in the process of being organised thus determinately incarnated. The focus here, from Marx's standpoint, would clearly be on the subtractive aesthetic process that the dynamic of organisation of works, genres, forms and so on incarnate in the determinateness of their emerging.

At this point, I would wish to insist once again that Muktibodh's oeuvre constitutes an unambiguous affirmation of his politico-aesthetic vision of literature being useful by virtue of it being a didacticism of desire, and the demonstration of continuous production as the actualisation of such instruction. And *Teesra Kshan* (The Third Moment) is an apt instantiation of that. In it Muktibodh (2002, pp. 14-15) has his friend Keshav say:

> *Iss baat per bahut kuch nirbhar karta hai ki aap kis sirey se baat shuru karenge. Yadi pathak, shrota ya darshak ke sirey se baat shuru karenge*

> *toh aapki vichar-yatra doosrey dhang kee hogi. Yadi lekhak ke sirey se sonchna shuru karenge toh baat alag prakar ki hogi. Dono sirey se baat hogi saundarya-mimansa kee hi. Kintu yatra kee bhinnata ke kaaran alag-alag raston ka prabhav vicharon ko bhinn banaa dega.*
>
> *Doh yatraon kee paraspar bhinnata, anivaarya roop se, paraspar-virodhi hai—yeh sonchna niraadhaar hai. Bhinnata poorak bhi ho sakti hai, virodhi bhi.*

(A lot depends on where you wish to start your argument from. If the argument begins from the standpoint of the reader, audience or spectator then the journey of your thinking will be of a certain kind. If you begin thinking from the writer's point of view then your argument will be different. In both instances, the argument will centre on aesthetic judgement. But because of the difference of the two journeys, the influence of their respectively different paths on thinking will render the two thought-processes different. To imagine that the mutual difference of the two journeys necessarily renders them mutually oppositional is without any basis. Difference can be complementary, it can be oppositional too.) [My translation.]

Here the poet's alter-ego is shown asserting that the two different approaches adopted respectively by the reader and the writer in analysing, and thus envisaging, the aesthetic process can be either mutually antagonistic or complementary, not necessarily just the former. As a result, the two approaches could, in their difference, also be *simultaneously* antagonistic and complementary to one another. But what exactly would this simultaneity of mutual antagonism and complementarity between the two different approaches of the reader and the writer with regard to the aesthetic process amount to? Grasped, for instance, from the reader's side, this would imply the reader affirms the writer by disavowing him. That is, the reader by disavowing the writer as the grammatical subject of the written work that constitutes determination vis-à-vis him tends to recommence the subtractive writing-as-process that the written work in its moment of emerging determinately incarnated and in thus incarnating interrupted. As a result, what the reader affirms in the process of disavowing the writer as the identitarian subject of the written work is the writer as the determinate subject-position—and thus grammatical subject—of the process of subtractive enunciation incarnated by the written work in its moment of becoming itself. Clearly, the writer as an identitarian subject, and the writer as the determinate subject-position of the process of subtractive enunciation are radically antagonistic. Now if we were to imagine Muktibodh's alter-ego Keshav himself as that reader, we could well say that since he, on account of his own readerly experience, grasps the difference in the approaches of the writer and reader as being both antagonistic and complementary, he would tend to see his own readerly move of disavowal of the determination of the written work as being constitutive of the recommencement of subtraction that the written work has interrupted in the process of determinately incarnating it. He would, therefore, also grasp such recommencement as affirmation of being-subtraction or subtractive ontology. In such a situation, he would, by virtue of being a reader, also simultaneously tend to be a writer. And since he would grasp his reader-becoming-writer move as the recommencement and thus affirmation of being-subtraction in a sustained fashion, he would, in the same movement of determinately recommencing subtraction (or writing-as-process as disavowal of determination of the written work), also prefigure the overcoming of his own authorial determination. Evidently, two things seem to be happening here. One, the reader grasps the written work of literature in terms of subtraction the latter determinately incarnated in its becoming itself as that written work, and thereby it disavows the identity and determination the written work is. This is indisputably a case of literature being rendered, by and for its reader, into a didacticism of desire and/or a generic truth-procedure. Two, literature, on account of the reader actualising its instruction of desire, becomes a generic field of interminable writing-as-process, or continuous production, and thus preclusion of distributively fixed division of labour between the writer and the reader.

However, the importance of *Teesra Kshan* (The Third Moment) as an affirmative manifesto of didacticism of desire and continuous production does not merely lie in the arguments it makes but, more significantly, in the form of the essay itself. The form of the Bakhtinian dialogue-as-polemical communication between the poet and his friend (or alter-ego), through which the text elaborates itself, is as powerful an affirmation of literature as a paradigmatic field of continuous production in its genericness as the arguments and propositions it discursively puts forth.

Unity of Dispersion: Epic Poetry, or Division of Labour Abolished

In the essay (2002, p. 29), *Ek Lambi Kavita ka Ant* (End of a Long Poem), Brechtian continuous production in the form of interminability of writing-as-process is sought to be further explicated with regard to the generic field of literature.

> *Idhar weh kavita mera pind nahin chord rahi thi. Agar weh kavita bhaavaaveshpurn hoti toh ek baar uski aaveshaatmak abhivyakti ho jane per meri chhutti ho jati. Lekin waisa ho sakna asambhav hai, kyunki bhaavaavesh kisee baat ko lekar hoti hai, weh baat kisee doosre baat se judi hoti hai, doosri baat kisee teesri baat se.*

(In here, that poem was unwilling to let go of me. Had that poem been full of passion, its emotional or affective expression would have meant my freedom from it. However, that was impossible, because passion is always with regard to something specific, and that specificity is, in turn, connected to another specificity and that another specificity is connected to yet another specificity.) [My translation.]

When seen through the prism of this excerpt, the scale and

form of an epic poem—and much of Muktibodh's poetry is just that—becomes a demonstration of what continuous production amounts to in the generic condition of art. This also, therefore, reveals why continuous production is a virtue of revolutionary aesthetics. The perpetual process of uninterrupted recommencement of desire is, in literature, revealed in and by the interminability of writing-as-process. And this interminability of writing-as-process is, in turn, formally effectuated, as Muktibodh seems to correctly observe, by the baggy proportions of an epic poem.

Such interminability of writing-as-process suggests that a work of literature *is*, only in its perpetual withdrawal from that which seeks to complete it. This means the written must interminably withdraw from itself by perpetually exceeding itself as writing-as-process to sustain that process which the written in its moment of coming into being had incarnated. It is this dialectically articulated modality of continuous production, specified as the interminability of writing-as-process in literature, that Blanchot (1989, pp. 22-23) indicates and affirms when he writes: "The writer writes a book, but the book is not yet the work. There is a work only when, through it, and with the violence of a beginning which is proper to it, the word *being* is pronounced. This event occurs when the work becomes the intimacy between someone who writes and someone who reads it. One might, then, wonder: if solitude is the writer's risk, does it not express the fact that he is turned, oriented toward the open violence of the work, of which he never grasps anything but the substitute—the approach and the illusion in the form of the book? The writer belongs to the work, but what belongs to him is only a book, a mute collection of sterile words, the most insignificant thing in the world. The writer who experiences this void believes only that the work is unfinished, and he thinks that a little more effort, along with some propitious moments, will permit him and him alone to finish it. So he goes back to work. But what he wants to finish by himself remains interminable; it involves him in an illusory task. And the work, finally, knows him not. It closes in around his absence as the impersonal, anonymous affirmation that it is—and nothing more." Blanchot's "being", which is conceptually central to his explication of the interminability of writing-as-process, is arguably derived from the Heideggerian philosophy of "ontological difference". It is, however, perfectly possible to set such metaphysical connotations aside and grasp "being", in this instance, simply as transcendental couching of the constellational construction posed and articulated by the uninterrupted process of dispersion that Brechtian continuous production is. And inasmuch as Brechtian continuous production is the abolition and preclusion of division of labour between the writer and the reader, it is an obviation of those identities of producer and consumer of the work. That renders the universe of work an "impersonal and anonymous affirmation that it is".

Blanchot (1989, pp. 22-23) further elaborates: "This is what is meant by the observation that the writer, since he only finishes his work at the moment he dies, never knows of his work. One ought perhaps to turn this remark around. For isn't the writer dead as soon as the work exists? He sometimes has such a presentiment himself: an impression of being ever so strangely out of work." Clearly, the interruption of the work—which as perpetual withdrawal is interminability of writing-as-process —by the written book is death of the writer. And, hence, the writer in embracing his death, and thus disavowing himself as the identitarian subject of the written book, finishes his work by clearing the way for the work in its withdrawal, or as interminability of writing-as-process, to recommence.

The unfolding of a poem, which is the operation of this interminability of writing-as-process in and as a specified literary form, is registered in Muktibodh as the effectuation of movement or flow of affects, and the narrative content of a poem is, for him, affective history. He (2002, p. 38) writes:

> *Kavita ke bheetar ki saari natakiyata vastutah bhavon kee gatimayata hai. Usi prakar, kavita ke bhitar ka katha-tatva bhi bhav ka itihas hai.*

(All the drama in a poem is practically the dynamic of affects. In the same way, the narrative content of a poem too is the history of affect.) [My translation.]

It is, therefore, hardly surprising that he (2002, p. 38) should envisage poetry as a form of dialectically articulated dispersive unity of "prose-images" (*gadya-chitra*). One which is recommencement of the processuality of dispersion due to its interruption by the very prose-images that in their emerging determinately incarnate its recommencement.

> *Toh phir aisee sthiti mey yeh asambhav nahin hai ki kavita ko anek krambadh gadya-chitron mey prastut kiya jaye. Athva anek krambadh gadya-chitra kuch iss tarah alokit aur deeptimaan ho uthen ki chhand ban jayen, gatimaan ho jayen aur ek vishesh disha ki ore pravahit ho saken.*

(So, in such a situation, it is not impossible to present a poem as a serialisation of many prose-images. Or, many series of prose-images are illumined and rendered radiant in a manner that rhyme comes out of them, they become dynamic and begin flowing in a particular direction.) [My translation.]

This shows that Muktibodh grasped poetry and envisaged his own poetic practice as an effectuation of the dynamic of recommencement of desire, which is the effectuation of being-subtraction, at the paradigmatic level of poetry as art.

Ethics of a Poet or a Politics of Poetry: Why Withdrawal is Not Subtraction

However, the essay does not stop there. It compels the artists to think the encounter between art and politics. It (2002, pp. 33-34) suggests the futility of art, literature and other similar critical intellectual vocations if the work of creating their own ethical condition of possibility is not integral to those vocations and pursuits.

> *Badey-badey aadarshvadi aaj Ravan ke yahan pani bharte hain, aur haan mey haan milate hain. Badey pragatisheel mahanubhaav bhi isi marj mey giraftaar hain. Jo vyakti Ravan ke yahan pani bharne se inkaar karta hai uskey bachche maare-maare phirte hain. Aur aap jante hain, ki khyatiprapt yashodeept pragatisheel mahanibhaav bhi (main sabki nahin keh sakta) un per hans padte hain ya kabhi-kabhi tuchch ke prati daya ke bhav se parilupt ho uthathe hain. Toh, sankshep mey, jo vyakti phatey haal aur phatichar hai, usey maanyata dene ki liye koi tayyar nahin, chaahe weh kitna hee naitik kyun na ho.*

[Great, well-known idealists are these days found slaving at Ravan's home, filling water, and busy being their master's voice. Many well-known progressive personalities are also in the grip of this ailment. An individual who refuses to fill water for Ravan has to see his children teeter precariously on the brink. And you know, how famous progressive personalities with halos of glory around their heads too (I can't speak for all) laugh at them or are filled with the kind of pity one feels for the lowly for them. So, in short, nobody is willing to grant recognition to a person whose existence is precarious, irrespective of how ethical that person might be.] (My translation.)

Clearly, the ethical condition of possibility of art, literature and other such critical intellectual vocations would be the universality of the truth of determinate subtraction—which those pursuits are in their emerging—in being-subtraction uninterruptedly.

Ethics, from Muktibodh's vantage-point as an artist, is the disavowal of the structure of exchange and relationality that art in its moment of subtractive emerging is a determinate incarnation of. Thus, the ethical condition of possibility of art as an activity for its own end, wherein art is not the object of determination of any extraneous condition, would be subtractive ontology as the ceaseless process constitutive of the simultaneity of infinite determinate subtractions. In other words, the ethical condition of possibility of art as an activity for its own end is the uninterrupted interminability of being-subtraction in, through and beyond art.

For, if art, literature and other such critical intellectual vocations do not have that work of universalisability as their integral condition of being, they are destined to assert and defend their sovereignty and thus lapse into and restore the very structure of exchange and relationality they tend to disavow in their emerging as art, literature and so on. This obviously means that art, literature and other intellectual vocations, their discursively articulated avowals of radicalism and revolutionary idealism notwithstanding, would be determined by, and thus dependent for their continuance on, the very capitalist structure of exchange that their discursively articulated declarations of radicalism and revolutionary idealism are meant to be a disavowal of. Clearly, sovereignty, even the sovereignty of the radical intellectual, is a chimera. This, as Muktibodh sees in such a clear-eyed fashion, is at the root of the rift between words and deeds, and the resultant hypocrisy and neurosis of radical intellectuals and artists. We must read his argument in *Ek Lambi Kavita ka Ant* (End of a Long Poem) as indicating how the assertion and defence of the sovereignty of identities and discursivities of radical intellectual and artistic projects—that is, their words—is precisely what causes their radicalism (in deed) to be undermined. He appears to understand very well that radicalism is not what radicalism says, but what radicalism does and keeps doing.

Therefore, it must be reiterated here yet again, that art, literature or any other similarly humanist intellectual vocation can hope to sustain the criticality and radicalism it determinately incarnates in its emerging, only by actively prefiguring the overcoming of the identity it would inevitably tend to lapse into on account of it being in its emerging a determinate incarnation of such radicalism and criticality. Any failure on that score would be the failure of that critical intellectual vocation to produce its own ethical condition of possibility. This condition would be the intersubjectivity of encounter—the mutual partaking of generic singularities—founding itself as its own subjective materiality of relationality of the nonrelational or continuous production.

And what is a fleeting affirmative gesture towards the ethical virtue of mutual partaking of generic singularities as continuous production—the uninterrupted simultaneity of infinite difference and infinite deployment of infinite difference —in *Ek Lambi Kavita ka Ant* (End of a Long Poem), becomes, in his poem *Bramharakshas* (1988, pp. 119-126), a clearly articulated statement of revolutionary transformation. It poses the question of abolition of art and politics as competing determinations constitutive of a stratified system of identities in order to actualise and preserve them as alterities (difference-as-its-own-deployment) or generic singularities.

In the final analysis, Muktibodh evidently has little use for pure ethics, something that his emphasis (in '*Ek Lambi Kavita ka Ant*') on the suffering of a person who steadfastly holds on to an ethical position might suggest. '*Bramharakshas*' is an unequivocal demonstration of that. Ethics, as far as Muktibodh's subjective disposition as a poet is concerned, is nothing more than politics as a yet-to-be realised materiality. One that will realise ethics in its materiality, thereby abolishing and precluding it. Which is to say that for an artist, and Muktibodh is one, ethics is grasping of the subtractiveness of art in its determinate emerging while politics is the infinitely sustained actuality of being-subtraction, or subtractive ontology.

Bramharakshas, the protagonist of the eponymous poem, is clearly someone who grasps his intellectual vocation in its determinate subtraction from the given structure and materiality of exchange and its correspondent intersubjectivity of relationality.

Bawdi kee un ghani gaharahiyon may shunya
Bramharakshas ek paitha hai,
va bheetar se umardti gunj kee bhi gunj,
bardbardahat-shabd pagal se.
Gahan anumanita
tan kee malinta
door karne ke liye pratipal
paap-chchaya door karne ke liye, din-raath
swachch karne –
Bramharakshas
ghis raha hai deh
haath ke panje, baraabar
banh-chchuti-muh chchapaachchap
khoob karte saaf,
phir bhi mael
phir bhi mael!!

Aur...honthon se
anokha strotra, koi kruddh mantrochchar,
athva shundh Sanskrit galiyon ka jwar,
mastak kee lakiren
bun rahin
alochanayon kay chamakte tar!!
Us akhand snan ka pagal pravah...
pran may samvedna hai syah!!

(In the blankness of the deep dark depths of the pond/lies a Bramharakshas,/And an echo of the echo bursting out from the inside,/like the words of an insane mutter./To rid himself, every moment, of grave doubts and his body of its squalid griminess/To rid himself of his sinful shadow/To cleanse himself/Brahmarakshas scrubs his body, day and night without any respite./His paws moving continuously over his arms-chest-face...splash! Splash! Splash!/To rub himself clean, absolutely clean,/Yet there's dirt/Yet there's grime!!

And...from his lips emanate bizarre shlokas, like some angry enunciation of spells,/or else, a torrent of invectives in impeccable Sanskrit,/the lines on his forehead/knitting together/shimmering threads of criticisms!!/The insane flow of that unceasing bath.../the blackness of his sensitive soul!!) [My translation.]

But in his endeavour to dwell in that subtractiveness, Bramharakshas ends up conflating (or hypostatising) the subtractive process his intellectual vocation in its emerging determinately incarnated, with the identity that his vocation, as a consequence, has lapsed into. Clearly, Bramharakshas reduces the non-discursive subtraction or the event—which is actualised in and as a determinate emerging but which is irreducible to the discursivity it, as a result, tends to lapse into —to the discursivised, identitarianised niche of his intellectual vocation only to dwell in it. As a result, subtractiveness from the given structure of exchange and relationality becomes, for Bramharakshas, an effort to lose the "sinful shadow, "dirt" and "grime" of the structure of exchange by withdrawing into the purported purity of his discursivised intellectual vocation. A vocation that in its putative discursivised purity consists of pronouncing "bizarre shlokas, like some angry enunciation of spells, or else, a torrent of invectives in impeccable Sanskrit with the lines on Bramharakshas' forehead knitting together shimmering threads of criticisms".

The question that the lines cited above rhetorically pose is, can a critical intellectual or radical artistic vocation (personified in Bramharakshas) retain its criticality and radicalism by seeking to keep that 'criticality' and 'radicalism' pure by purporting to stand apart from the impure world and obsessively working towards holding that world and its impurities at bay? Does that not make such a vocation or project complicit in maintaining and perpetuating the very impure world with which it wants to have nothing to do? Does not Bramharakshas' purity, which he seeks to attain by obsessively washing himself of the shadow of sin, and all the dirt and grime of the world around by seeking to keep himself separate from that world, render him complicit in its perpetuation as the dump of sin, grime and dirt it is? For, is it not this obsession of his to remain pure that prevents Bramharakshas from wading into its dirt and grime to wipe it out and thus perpetuates all that grime and dirt and makes his supposed purity complicit and part of it?

Little does he realise that subtraction is not withdrawal from the structure of exchange and relationality but its disavowal and destruction through the generalisation of subtractiveness as and into subtractive ontology. To mistake withdrawal for subtraction is to do what an anarchist such as Proudhon or the "utopian socialists" proposed and/or tried to accomplish. Such withdrawal cannot *be* because by disengaging with the structure of exchange and relationality it implies leaving the latter intact, together with its objective wont to rearticulate that which seeks to withdraw from it. This is just what Marx and Engels demonstrated through their respective critiques of Proudhon (in *The Poverty of Philosophy*) and "utopian socialists" (in *Anti-Duehring*). Rather, subtractive ontology as the mode that materialises itself as the uninterrupted simultaneity of infinite difference and infinite deployment of infinite difference is in radical antagonism to the structure of exchange, its materiality of social division of labour and its correspondent intersubjectivity of relationality. This should leave none in any doubt that the destruction or unravelling of the structure/mode of exchange is integral to becoming-subtraction, or subtractive ontology.[4]

Be that as it may, from the position of pure ethics—which is clearly the one constitutive of the Bramharakshas subjectivity —withdrawal is equated with subtraction. The wont of a position that is purely ethical is to dwell, at a subjective level, in the subtractiveness that art or other similarly critical intellectual vocations determinately incarnate in their emerging even as those vocations are, objectively speaking, subsumed within and articulated by the structure of exchange and relationality. This ensures that subject-positions of pure ethics, even when those positions are so in complete good faith, must unwittingly accept the value that gets ascribed to their subjective dwelling in the subtractiveness of their different critical intellectual vocations by way of valorisation of their objectively identitarianised correlates. This happens because such identitarianisation, which the fact of their interruption as singularities wreaks on them, restores the structure of exchange and its logic of valorisation. Clearly, the subjective dwelling in the emerging subtractiveness of critical intellectual vocations, and the purely ethical subject-positions constitutive of such dwelling, remain neither subtractive nor, therefore, ethical. There is something, no matter how unequal, that the purely ethical subject-position of Bramharakshas gains in exchange for the pain he suffers in withdrawing into the niche of his 'critical' intellectual vocation from the structure of exchange. Worse, he even comes to accept and take pride in what he gets, maintaining his suffering, and dwelling in it as a kind of symbolic capital of pain. The structure of exchange pays him with awe and respect mixed with terror and derision for the suffering it extracts from him on account of his withdrawal from it in order to be the apparently intransigent, lone, secluded intellectual or artist that he is. Those who inhabit the subjectivity of pure ethics in all good faith rest content with that. While those who come to do so in bad faith seek to, and often succeed, in realising that value of awe and respect mixed with derision and terror as a very good price in the capitalist society and economy constitutive of the structure/mode of exchange and valorisation.

That is exactly what the poet, who figures in the poem as its narrative voice, tells us about Bramharakshas:

Kintu, gahri bawdi
kee bheetree deewar per
tirchi giree Ravi-rashmi
ke udte huye parmanu, jab
tal tak pahunchte hain kabhi
tab Bramharakshas samajhta hai, Surya nay
jhukkar 'Namaste' kar diya.
Path bhoolkar jab chandni
kee kiran takraye kahin deewar per,
tab Bramharakshas samajhta hai
vandana kee chandni nay
gyan-guru maanaa usey.

(But, if and when some stray atoms of the sunbeam,/which falls a-slant on the inner walls that enclose the deep pond,/reach its bottom/Bramharakshas takes that to be the sun's wish to bow before him in obeisance./If ever moonlight, straying from its path,/collides with those walls,/Bramharakshas is given to believe that the moon,/which has accepted him as its master,/ is singing paeans to him.) [My translation.]

That is certainly not subtraction. But is it, for that matter, even a successful withdrawal from the structure of exchange and its correspondent intersubjectivity of relationality? Can there ever be a withdrawal that succeeds? Is 'successful withdrawal' not a paradox, a Kantian antinomy, as it were? Does a good-faith ethical subject, even at the level of its purely subjective experience, really dwell in the subtractiveness from the structure of exchange his intellectual vocation in its emerging had determinately incarnated as a subjective materiality? Evidently, the good-faith ethical subject such as Bramharakshas is, from Muktibodh's standpoint of radical aesthetics, as much responsible for the perpetuation of the structure of exchange and relationality as the bad-faith ethical subjects whom we have seen him scorn as Ravan's slaves in *Ek Lambi Kavita ka Ant* (End of a Long Poem).

Kintu yug badla va aaya keerti-vyavsayi
...labhkari karya me se dhan,
va dhan may se hriday-man,
aur, dhan-abhibhoot antahkaran may se
satya kee jhain
nirantar chilchilatee thi.
Atmachetas kintu is
vyaktitva may thi pranmai anban...
vishwachetas be-banav!!
Mahatta ke charan may tha
vishadakul man!
Mera usi se un dinon hota Milan yadi
toh vyatha uski swyam jeekar
batataa mai usey uska swyam ka mulya
uskee mahatta!
Va us mahatta ka
hum sareekhon ke liye upyog,
us aantarikta ka batataa mai mahatva!!

Pis gaya veh bheetree
au' baharee doh kathin paton beech,
aisee tragedy hai neech!!

(But the epoch changed, and traders of fame arrived/...in profitable activity shimmered wealth,/while only in that wealth could heart-and-mind be glimpsed,/and, the brightness of truth flashed unceasingly from the inner recesses of a soul overwhelmed by such riches./But in this self-conscious/being resided life-affirming contradictions.../an unreconstructed consciousness of the world!! On the feet of greatness lay prostrate/a despairing soul!/If only I had met with him then/ I would surely have lived his pain/to tell him his own value/ his greatness!

Also, the use such greatness could be put to/for people like us,/And the significance of such inwardness I would surely have communicated to him!!/But alas, it ended in a lowly tragedy!/Caught as he was between the inner and outer mill stones of his dilemma that ground him to dust!!) [My translation.]

This part of the poem is a savagely brilliant demonstration of how Bramharakshas, the subject of pure ethics, in allowing himself to be subsumed by the structure of exchange and relationality is eventually crushed by it. Bramharakshas' purely ethical position drives him, as we have seen, to dwell, at a subjective level, in the subtractiveness that his critical intellectual vocation had determinately incarnated in its emerging even as that subtractiveness has lapsed to become, at an objective level, an identity. This interruptive transformation of a determinate subtraction into an identity restores the structure of exchange into which it lapses, and which as a result valorises it. Clearly, Bramharakshas, impelled by his purely ethical quest, dwells in a chimera of withdrawal from the structure of exchange that, objectively speaking, is a perpetuation of precisely that structure and its constitutive logic of valorisation. Evidently, it is Bramharakshas' pure ethicality that ensures his defeat by the dialectical cunning of the structure of exchange and valorisation, which then finishes him off.

Bramharakshas is first trapped in a web of valorisation and thus competing determinations, which then goes on to endanger his intellectual vocation, his spirit and, eventually, his very existence. The capitalist structure of exchange and relationality, as long as it is around as an objective fact, is destined by the sheer fact of such existence to define everything that comes into being in relation to itself. That results in such determinately subtractive activity to be identitarianised and thus undermined as the subtraction its coming into being is. However, the subsumption of the undermined or lapsed subtraction by the structure, which, dialectically speaking, is restored in that lapse, then tends to finish off such lapsed subtractions; or identities, value-forms or commodities. For, what purpose or end can a purportedly critical intellectual or artistic identity or commodity that in its discursivity still continues to disavow exchange and valorisation have within and for the structure of exchange and valorisation in a situation where the latter's scope has hugely expanded? Bramharakshas' intellectual vocation and his soul are, as the poem here shows us, doubtless caught in an extremely painful situation of being constantly threatened with extinction. But it also demonstrates this to be the logical culmination of his subsumption by the structure of exchange and relationality, not despite but because of his purely ethical quest to withdraw from that structure into the niche of his 'critical' intellectual calling. The subtractiveness that Bramharakshas' intellectual vocation was in its emerging, and his purely ethical position, both cease to be themselves, paradoxically, on account of the pure ethicality of his position and subjective orientation. The ethical Bramharakshas, in seeking to withdraw from the structure of exchange and relationality by way of his critical intellectual vocation, tends to render such withdrawal into an assertion and defence of the sovereignty of his intellectual vocation. And sovereignty is pyrrhic because its success implies the restoration of the structure of identity, exchange and relationality, which subsumes it as that sovereignty to undermine it. The ethical Bramharakshas is, therefore, unmistakably complicit in his own suffering and death. And for that reason such suffering and extinction are correctly characterised in the poem as a "lowly tragedy" (*aisee tragedy hai neech!!!*).

Affirmation by Disavowal: A Dialectic for the Singular

But it is here the poet steps in as the narrative voice he is in the poem to affirm Bramharakshas by disavowing him. This simultaneity of affirmation and disavowal is articulated by the poet by affirming Bramharakshas' greatness on account of the pain the latter had to suffer because of his withdrawal into the niche of his intellectual vocation from the structure of exchange and relationality. However, this affirmation is articulated in terms of the use [*upyog*], and the value (*moolya*) thereof, that such "greatness" has for "people like us". Clearly, this affirmation of the use and value of Bramharakshas' pain and suffering "for people like us" is an affirmation of the determinate subtraction that his critical intellectual subjectivity of withdrawal from the structure of exchange incarnated in its emerging. It is, therefore, an affirmation that is shown to be possible only in, as and through the disavowal of Bramharakshas, who is the lapsed subtraction and the subsumed subject of the structure of exchange and relationality. This lapsed subtraction, and identitarianised and subsumed subject no longer knows its own subtractiveness (and use-value thereof) in ceasing to become it. The affirmation of Bramharakshas' greatness, and pain and suffering, the poet correctly points out, is possible and useful only through the recommencement of its subtractive condition with the poet himself living it in his own time. Only that would constitute a real affirmation of Bramharakshas' greatness, and his pain and suffering as a use-value that, in the same movement, would be disavowal of the twinned subsumed identities of Bramharakshas' subjectivity of withdrawal and his intellectual vocation that is the valorised objective correlate of that subjectivity.

In a work of Biblical hermeneutics from a revolutionary-proletarian standpoint, Negri (2009, pp. xix-xx) writes: "Job had been loyal to all measures that regulated the world supported by God; the workers had been loyal to all the measures that regulated the world governed by capital. Now, though, measure had exploded. Job protested against measure and he suffered from the pain of the incommensurability of life: now all measure had blown up. What has all this to do with my anxiety for liberation? The reason is minor and simple but also profound: both the workers' movement and I experienced what Job had, that is, the pain of incommensurability and the consequent discovery that to the end of measure one could reply only with the passion of creation. Where old measures had fallen it was necessary to create new ones; and passion could only play itself out now in the capacity to move with joy beyond measure. Only from this perspective was it possible to imagine communism anew."

The whole point of affirming pain and suffering, in this context, is not to preserve them and thereby give them a measure, no matter how unequal, for existing as that pain and suffering. Rather, the point of such affirmation, which is essentially affirmation of the condition of incommensurability and subtractiveness that such pain and suffering in coming into being determinately actualise, is to generalise that condition of immeasurability and subtraction through transvaluation of pain, and the concomitant disavowal of measure and exchange, into an immensity of "joy beyond measure" and "passion for creation".

The poet in affirming Bramharakshas' greatness in terms of his suffering and pain, by simultaneously disavowing Bramharakshas in his ethical dwelling in the facticity of such pain and suffering, is seeking to "create new ones (measures)" of use-value "where the old measures..." of exchange-based valorisation "...had fallen", thereby attempting to make it "possible to imagine communism anew" in, as and through the determinate recommencement of subtraction and its universalisability into and as the subjective materiality of relationality of the nonrelational, or the uninterrupted simultaneity of infinite difference and infinite deployment of infinite difference.

Thus the poet's affirmation of Bramharakshas' pain is not

in terms of the capitalist structure visiting it on the sufferer, but in terms of the subtractive condition of Bramharakshas in his moment of pre-identitarian emerging. The meaning that Bramharakshas gives to his pain in suffering it is bound to his subjective identity and the equally identitarianised objective correlate of his intellectual vocation, and thus has a measure and a value within the structure of exchange it as an identity incarnates. That is something we have seen the poem demonstrate in order to disavow. To that extent, the pain and suffering of Bramharakshas—which is the subtractive condition and moment of his coming into being—that the poet affirms, is in radical antagonism to the facticity of pain and suffering that Bramharakshas inhabits as a subjective identity correspondent with his intellectual vocation as an equally identitarianised objective correlate.

This asymmetrical—or singular—dialectic between subtraction that Bramharakshas was an incarnation of in his moment of emerging and the identity that he has become, and whose sovereignty he ends up asserting in hypostatically 'affirming' the subtraction he had incarnated in the moment of his coming into being, is most clearly evident in the last stanza of the poem:

Vah jyoti anjaani sada ko so gayee
yah kyon hua!
Kyon yah hua!!
Mai Bramharakshas ka sajal-ur shishya
hona chahta
jisse ki uska adhoora karya,
uskee vedna ka srot
sangat, purna nishkarshon talak
pahuncha sakoon.

(That light has been snuffed out for ever/Why! Oh why! Did this have to happen!/I now wish to become/the truest disciple of Bramharakshas/so that I can take his unfinished task,/the source of his pain,/closer to its fully logical conclusions.) [My translation.]

Clearly, Bramharakshas' discipleship that the poets wishes to adopt, while grieving his death, is all about affirming the subtractive condition of Bramharakshas' pain and suffering by recommencing it and its universalisability by living it in his own determinateness, thus taking his unfinished (or interrupted) task to its logical conclusion. Such affirmation of Bramharakshas as the incarnation of subtraction or unleashing of desire that he was in his emerging, which is thus constitutive of disavowal of Bramharakshas as the valorised subjective identity he consequently becomes, shows that Bramharakshas' instruction for the poet-as-his-disciple is the instruction of desire. Therefore, Bramharakshas, as the persona-effect of a radical intellectual and/or aesthetic project that the poem shows him to be, renders such a vocation or project a generic truth-procedure.

And what such a disciple of Bramharakshas would be to Bramharakshas, the dead rebel in his afterlife is to his former living self in '*Ek Bhootpoorva Vidrohi ka Atmakathan*' (The Autobiography of a Former Rebel) (1988, pp. 49-57). This poem is the voice of a former rebel speaking from beyond the grave. And by virtue of being that voice and what it enunciates, the poem comes across as afterlife, in Benjamin's sense of the term, of the former rebel. Here we get to encounter this afterlife as the affirmation and recommencement of subtraction that was determinately incarnated by the rebel's rebellion in his former life. That this determinate subtraction failed to grasp itself thus, and was hence unable to prefigure the overcoming of identity it consequently became due to the interruption of that subtraction, is the reason why it was destined only to be a rebellion, not revolution. That is the reason why the *rebellion* of the former rebel is seen, from the vantage-point of its afterlife that is the poem in question, as subsumed and thus trapped within the system it rebels against. Such subsumption is not despite the rebellion but because it is no more than a rebellion, which in its determinately subtractive eruption was unreflexive and was, therefore, inevitably interrupted. Hence, we get to see, from the vantage-point of his afterlife, how the former rebel is a partial revolutionary and his rebellion an incomplete revolution.

The afterlife of the rebel affirms the subtraction that the rebellion of his former life determinately incarnated in its moment of emerging. In the same movement, his afterlife also becomes a disavowal of the structure of exchange that was restored by the identitarianised former rebel self of his due to lapse of the subtraction its rebellion had, in the moment of its breaking out, determinately incarnated. This rebel in his afterlife, therefore, also understands and accepts, as he seems to be telling us here, that his disavowal of the structure of exchange also entails, in the same movement, the death and destruction of his former rebel self and its life.

And in tending to be that which they affirm, the dead rebel and his lapsed revolution in their twinned afterlives tend to become what they were (already no longer as not yet): subtraction, albeit now in its becoming as uninterrupted processuality. Clearly, the rebel, and his rebellion, in their twinned afterlives, is what Marx would have called "revolution in permanence". This revolution is shown here to recognise itself in its earlier incomplete life embodied by rebels and rebellions in their unreflexive and thus interrupted moments of determinately subtractive eruption. Hence, what the revolution recognises as itself in its incomplete forelife are not names and identities of rebels or rebellions, or such identitarianising features as their fame, but the pictures of the anonymous nonidentitarian processuality that is the internal constitutivity of identities of rebels and rebellions that in being those identities tend to conceal or repress such nonidentity and yet reveal it as its symptoms.

> *Puraana makan tha, dhehna tha, dheh gaya,*
> *bura kya hua?*
> *Badey-badey dhrinrdaakaar dambhvaan*
> *khambe wey dheh padey!!*
> *Jardibhoot parton mey, avashya hum dub gaye!*
> *Hum unmey rah gaye,*
> *Bura hua, bahut bura hua!!*
> *Prithvi ke pet mey ghuskar jab*
> *Prithvi ke hriday kee garmi ke dwara*
> *mitti ke dher ye chattan bun jayenge*
> *toh un chattanon kee*
> *aantarik parton kee satah mey*
> *chitra ubhar ayenge*
> *hamare chehre ke, tan-badan ke, sharir ke,*
> *Antar kee tasveereyen ubhar aayengi, sambhavtah,*
> *Yahi ek aasha hai kee*
> *mitti ke andhere un*
> *itihas-staron mey tab*
> *hamara bhi chinnh reh jayega.*
> *Naam nahin,*
> *Kirti nahin,*
> *Kewal avshesh, Prithvi ke khodey huye gaddhon mey*
> *rahasyamay purushon ke panjar aur*
> *jung-khayee nokon ke astra!!*

(It was an old house, it had to fall apart, it fell apart,/What is bad about that?/Huge, haughty, determined,/those pillars came crashing down!!/In stratified layers we certainly got stuck!/We remained in them/That was bad, really very bad!!/When in the bowels of the earth/all this debris becomes rock/due to the warmth of the earth's heart/then on the surface of the layers/in the innermost recesses of those rocks/pictures will emerge/of our visages, bodies and anatomies,/Photographs of our interiors will also probably emerge/There is only this hope/ then that those dark history-layers of the soil/will be marked by our signs too./Not name,/not fame,/Only remnants, in the dug-out trenches of the earth/of skeletons of mysterious men and/weapons with rusted edges!!) [My translation.]

Of Lapsed Revolutions and Literary Myths: For a Muktibodhian Alternative

Muktibodh increasingly found himself confined to the level of literature, thanks to the growing difficulty he encountered in finding appropriate opportunities to actualise his commitment as a practising militant of communist politics. His confinement to literature appeared, as an objective fact, to be merely a particularity, but, insofar as Muktibodh's very own experience and practice were concerned, this level of literature to which he found himself confined was a generic singularity. The effects of his literary practice, and the subjective experience that animated such practice, leave very little scope for doubt on that score. The question that we, therefore, need to ask is, was Muktibodh able to fulfil his desire of becoming Bramharakshas' truest and most accomplished disciple, or was he Bramharakshas himself? Did he become the revolutionary fulfilment of rebellions in their afterlife, or did he stay a mere rebel, a lapsed revolutionary?

Extensive biographical information has been mined and marshalled, often with great archival rigour, by Muktibodh scholars and legions of leftwing critics to demonstrate the intransigence of his commitment both as a poet and a political militant. It is, therefore, indisputable that he was no Bramharakshas, but what he aspired in the eponymous poem to be: Bramharakshas' truest disciple.

However, what we would do well here to focus our attention on is how did that pain and restlessness, which Muktibodh suffered in his life on account of his intransigent struggle to remain true to his commitment as a practising political militant, shape his literature. In other words, how can we discern from that literature itself—not only by what his poems and prose say at a declarative level but more by virtue of how and what they are at the level of their formal organisation—and with no reference whatsoever to his biography, that he was no lapsed revolutionary? Or, a Bramharakshas proposing literature as a realm to withdraw into on account of the difficulty to continue with the project of actualising his commitment as a practising militant of radical politics?

Muktibodh inhabited, as much in life as in his art, an alternative reality. Harishankar Parsai (2011, p. 315), while reminiscing about his friendship with the poet, writes:

> *Mrityu se doh saal pehle vey Jabalpur aaye thhey. Raat-bhar vey bardbardate thhey. Ek raat cheekhkar khaat se farsh per gir padey. Sambhale, tab bataayaa ki ek bahut badi chhipkali sapne mey sir per gir rahi thi.*

(Two years before his death, he had come to Jabalpur. All through the night he would keep muttering and mumbling in his sleep. One particular night he screamed and fell down from the bed. Once he managed to get his wits about him he said he had dreamt of a huge house-lizard falling on his head.) [My translation.] This demonstrates the intensity and the sense of palpable authenticity with which Muktibodh dwelt in the reality of such dreams and fantasies. And that is exactly the reason why Muktibodh repeatedly shows himself confronting such reality, expressed in the darkly weird and horror-inducing imagery of his poetry, as its grammatical poet-subject. But for Muktibodh this alternative reality is not, as the surrealistic discursivity or identity of his poetic imagery might seem to suggest, a mythic universe of fantasy and literature into which he could withdraw from the 'realist' historical reality he found himself in. The strangeness and unfamiliarity of the imagery of his poems does not seek to arrest the reader in the surrealistic and/or fantastic discursivity of its appearance. Instead, such imagery, in his poems, discernibly demonstrate the expressionistic force that animates them and of which they are incarnations.

The expressionistic style, diction and voice of his poetry—and the epic scale and form of most of his poems that such expressionism effectuates—render his poems, as the organisation of the surrealistic imagery they are at the level of their discursive appearance, demonstrations of their own performativity or gesticness. As a result, the weird, unfamiliar, horror-inducing reality of his poetic world, constitutive of the discursivity of its surrealistic imagery, demonstrates itself as the subjective-materiality of being-subtraction. So, even as Muktibodh, the individual, is forced by circumstances to confine himself to the determinate level of literature, Muktibodh, the grammatical-subject of his literature, envisages literature as problematising itself as the paradigmatic abstraction it is. Therefore, Muktibodh's poetic world is not mythic and ahistorical. Rather, the alternative reality he inhabited, and which is embodied in his poetry, has a historicity. It is the historicity of sustained being of subtraction or continuous production, and thus a historicity of suspension of history and the historical. The term "historicity without history" (Bosteels, 2009, p. xiv) is meant to conceptualise just this kind and mode of alternative reality.

In this, Muktibodh is a radical contrast to his Bramharakshasian contemporaries and successors, some of them practitioners of "Nayee Kavita" (new poetry) and "Nayee Kahani" (new story), whose literature is arguably constitutive of alternative reality as self-enclosed worlds of static strangeness and unfamiliarity, and are thus myths. Such literature, therefore, proposes itself as a disavowal of the determination by historical reality in its givenness only to be itself embraced as yet another determination of an alternative world of literature unto itself. It constitutes a proposal for passive defamiliarisation as movement from one enchantment, which is that of the historical, into another, which is that of the mythical. It can be called, following Lefebvre's (1992, p. 112) criticism of Surrealism, "a skilfully organized confusion between 'permanent revolution' and permanent scandal". Hence, what such literature proposes about itself, through the performativity that its form renders discernible, is withdrawal, not subtraction. Something from which the subtraction it determinately incarnated in its moment of emerging can be recovered by a Brechtian, or a Muktibodhian, reader but which such literature in its own discursivised non-reflexivity does not at all propose for itself.

Such literature of withdrawal is incomplete disavowal of determination. For, disavowal of determination is really the disavowal of interruption of subtraction on account of its determinate actualisation. Such disavowal is not meant to be conflated with or reduced to its appearance, which is negation of the identitarianised determination that a lapsed subtraction manifests itself as. Therefore, a complete disavowal of determination—insofar as it is disavowal of the interruption of subtraction, and its concomitant recommencement for universalisability—must consist of the negation of a given determination (historical reality in the instant case) simultaneously prefiguring the negation of the determination or identity (literature as myth here) that the first negation will tend to lapse into.

In that sense, withdrawal from a given identitarianised determination into another identity, and hence determination, is no different from the move of an identity to triumph over its determination by another identity to determine the latter in turn. Withdrawal from and triumph over an identitarianised determination are merely two different registers for thinking and envisaging negation of determination as yet another determination, which is the constitutive principle of the structure of exchange and relationality. Hence, they can be called two sides of the same Hegelian, or capitalist, coin of constitutive antitheses.

Beyond the Exchange Principle: The Wager of Subtraction

Subtraction from, disavowal of and radical antagonism towards the structure of exchange and relationality is a theme and an engagement that runs like a thread through Muktibodh's work giving it its unity. It figures not only as the assertive-discursive aspect of his literature but, more importantly, as the formal, digetic and performative dimensions of it as well. One of the most clear statements on that score are constituted by these oft-quoted stanzas of *Andherey Mey* (In the Darkness) (1988, pp. 126-171):

...O merey aadarshvaadi mann,
Aur merey siddhantvaadi mann,
Ab tak kya kiya?
Jeevan kya jiya!!
Udranbhari bun anaatm bun gayey,
Bhhoton kee shadi mey kanaat se tan gayey,
Kisi vyabhichar ke bun gayey bistar,

Dukhon ke dagon ko tamgon-sa pehna,
Apne hi khayalon mey din-raat rehna,
Asang buddhi va akele mey sahna
Zindagi nishkriya bun gayi talghar,

Aab tak kya kiya,
Jeevan kya jiya!!
Bataao toh kis-kiske liye tum daud gayey
Karuna ke drishyon se hai! Muh mord geyey,
Bun gayey patthar;

Bahut-bahut jyada liya,

Diya bahut-bahut kam;
Mar gaya desh, aarey, jeevit rah gayey tum!!

("...Oh my idealist soul,/And my philosophical soul,/What have you done up until now?/What has been your life!!/In your self-obsession you have been un-selfed,/To be stretched into a marquee at the wedding feast of ghosts,/To become the bed of some lechery,

Signs of grief you sport like medals,/To live day and night in your own thoughts,/In your incoherent intelligence you suffer alone/Life has become a vegetative basement,

What have you done up until now,/What has been your life!!/Name me those to whose aid you rushed/Fie on you! for having turned away from scenes of compassion,/To become a stone

You have taken a lot,/Given very little in return,/The land is dead, only you are left alive!!) [My translation.]

It is, indeed, quite unfortunate that these stanzas, especially the last, are predominantly read merely as a criticism of the phenomenon of well-established 'radical' intellectuals and artists getting along well in their lives and their vocations, even as the world around them falls apart, by taking a lot and giving very little in return. Such a psychologised reading—arguably through the biographical prism of the pain that Muktibodh as an individual suffered in his life on account of his uncompromising and steadfast political commitment—has made those lines out to be simply the resentful cry of an individual suffering due to the intransigence of his commitment. Worse, through such a reading, those last three lines have been transformed into a sort of progressive-radical credo. This tends to suggest that radicalism is all about the resentful assertions of committed activists and artists on being denied their due by the system. While reading those stanzas in such terms, it does not occur to us what would a radicalism that articulates itself as resentment for being denied its due by the system amount to? Can the system give what is due to radicalism? And if that be so would radicalism as the demand for the impossible, really be itself? Would radicalism, by virtue of envisaging itself as the *ressentiment* of suffering people, and thus rendering itself a project of placing its demands before the system for the latter to fulfil them, be anything more than reformism? Doesn't such a reading imply that those lines are radical because they are somehow invested in reforming the unreformed structure of exchange and relationality?

It must be stated here that such a biographical and psychologised reading of those stanzas is grossly mistaken about its 'radical' self-image. Such reading is actually quite reactionary. That such a reading should be in vogue is, however, not surprising. Such a way of seeing and reading arguably stems from radical literature and politics having been reduced to the status of moral and moralising vocations and projects.

The truth is those four stanzas in question are highly radical for reasons that are the absolute opposite of those suggested by the aforementioned reading of it. Those stanzas constitute a sharp exposition of how the quest to preserve and assert the sovereignty of the self—possibly in order to affirm subtraction of whose actuality the self is a determinate historical index – is precisely what robs the self of its selfhood. More pertinently, it reveals the self for the chimera of autonomy and sovereignty that it *is* in its historically subjectivated and/or identitarianised existence as that self.

Hence, when the poet-subject of the poem is found ruing his "idealist and ideologically-committed soul" for having "taken a lot" and "given back very little" he is by no means exhorting well-established 'radical' intellectuals and artists to give back a little more and take a little less. Instead, those lines clearly suggest that in a situation structured by the exchange-principle there will always be some who take more and give less and others who will, thereby, be compelled to take less and give more. He is lamenting the fact that the structure of exchange he is caught in is constitutively unreformable.

Any Marxist worth his salt should know that the principle of equal exchange is constitutively unequal insofar as equal exchange takes place between mutually unequal subject-positions (of capital and labour) and reproduces that inequality. Equal exchange has primitive accumulation as its constitutive condition of possibility that is concealed in the factuality of equal exchange. The fact of equal exchange between the mutually unequal subject-positions of labour and capital, wherein the labour gives what it can and gets in return from capital what it deserves for giving what it could, tends to mask the fact of how labour and capital, with their mutually unequal capacities to give and take respectively, come into being and are reproduced. In other words, the embodiment of the principle of equal exchange tends to mask how its underlying structure—which is capital as a relation constitutive of valorisation of labour-power or valorisation or productive extraction of surplus labour-time—comes into being and is reproduced.

So, while the poet-subject is doubtless scathing in the (self-) criticism of his "idealist" and "ideologically-committed" soul, the vehemence of such criticism is not individualised and moral but systemic and political. The individualised, and thus moral, register through which such political critique is ineluctably articulated, given that it is in the form of poetry, must not blind us to what such criticism actually amounts to. The poet-subject condemns his idealist and ideologically-committed soul for having become the "marquee" at the "wedding feast of ghosts" and "the bed of lechery" precisely in trying to preserve and assert its sovereignty. This is a critique that before being what it appears as—the individualised condemnation of lapsed radical artists and intellectuals—is a demonstration of how interrupted subtractions, on account of their unreflexivity, mistake the assertion and defence of the sovereignty of their identities for the affirmation of subtraction they determinately incarnated in their non-identitarian moment of emerging.

Those stanzas in question, therefore, imply the determinate recommencement of subtraction and its universalisability, and the concomitant disavowal of its prior interruption, and the decimation of the structure of exchange that is incarnated in such interruption. It is such recommencement of subtraction and its universalisability as continuous production that the poem performatively demonstrates through its expressionistic diction and voice, and its excruciatingly endless epic length. The following lines from the last part of the poem constitute an unambiguous assertion on that score:

> *Pratyek vastu ka nij-nij alok,*
> *Maano ki alag-alag phoolon ke rangeen*
> *alag-alag vaatavaran hain bemaap,*
> *Pratyek arth kee chaya mey doosra, aashai*
> *jhilmila raha-sa.*

(Every object in its respective light,/As if, they are all incommensurable,/like differently coloured environments of different flowers,/In the shadow of every meaning, the sense of the other/seems to shimmer.) [My translation.]

Every object is grasped in the poem as the measure-disavowing, desire-unleashing subtractiveness it determinately was in its respective moment of emerging, and not as the identity or value-form it is in the given system of history constitutive of the structure of exchange and relationality. As a result, the poem sees and shows how in the shadow of *meaning* of every such object the sense of all the others shimmers connotatively. In such circumstances, every object, in its respective nonidentitarianness, is didacticism or instruction of desire for every other object. Which is why the poem, in grasping all those objects as existing in and as non-exchange and nonrelationality vis-à-vis one another, tends to affirm and actualise them as such. That is to say, it itself demonstrably tends to become the actuality of such simultaneity of mutuality and nonrelationality, or, more accurately, mutual partaking of generic nonrelationalities or singularities. That would be subtractive ontology or universal-singularity as the uninterrupted simultaneity of infinite difference and infinite deployment of infinite difference. In concrete practice, this would amount to the interminable process of continuous production as the unravelling of the materiality of social division of labour, its intersubjectivity of relationality, and their constitutive structure of exchange.

However, the question that needs to be asked here is, why does or should one decide to grasp an object not as the identity it is in its empirical givennness? What is the philosophical basis for taking such a decision? Why should such a decision be taken at all? We would do well here to clarify this philosophical question with reference to the genericness of art. That would, among other things, be in keeping with Muktibodh's politico-aesthetic vision of inflecting idea with desire.

What we, therefore, need to pointedly ask is, why should we grasp art as subtraction from the ontological horizon or structure of exchange and relationality, and not simply as the identitarianised negation of determination of non-art it apparently is? That is because, tendentially speaking, subtraction arguably has primacy over negation. This contention derives from the fact that determination is logically consequent to negation. That is to say, one negates a determination, first and foremost, to determinately overcome necessity and only then to be a new level of determination or necessity in turn. Thus, the tendential primacy of exceeding necessity, over constitution of a new level of necessity yet again, is also the primacy of the tendency of contingency over that of necessity. To envisage and assert this tendential primacy as a generality is to pose and/or actualise a new order of affirmation of "necessity of contingency". Subtraction is this new affirmation, this new generality in its incipient, tendential form.

This, among other things, also demonstrates that to grasp art as negation of determination, and not subtraction, would be idealism. That is because it amounts to art being grasped in terms of a pre-assigned place within the structure or ontological horizon of alternation of negation and determination. Clearly, such symmetry, even when there is motion and dialectic, is integral to idealism. Which is exactly the case when the emerging of art through the negation of determination of non-art, which resists such emerging, leads us to grasp the meaning or destiny of art in terms of it being yet another determination. That is because the meaning of art as simply what it appears to be—which is the negation of determination of non-art to thus be a determination in its own right (the sovereignty of art)—is subject to the structural law of alternation of negation and determination. This means the law of the structure is antecedent or a priori to the emerging of art.

Yet, just because every constitutive moment of becoming-subtraction is inescapably determinate in its subtractiveness, its universalisable actualisation is always fraught with the peril of the unreflexivity of its determinately constitutive subject-positions. A peril that manifests itself in the lapse of a determinate subtraction into an identity. Muktibodh, as the following lines reveal, is perfectly aware of that:

> *Ek-a-ek veh vyakti...*
> *Samne*
> *galiyon mey, sardkon per, logon kee bheerd mey*
> *chala ja raha hai.*
> *Dharakta hai dil*
> *ki pukarne ko khulta hai muh*
> *ki aksmaat...*
> *Veh dikha, veh dikha*
> *veh phir kho gaya kisi jan-yooth mey...*

> *Uthi huyee banh yah uthi huyee rah gayee!!*
>
> *An-khoji nij samriddhi ka veh param utkarsh,*
> *Param abhivyakti...*
> *Main uska shishya hoon*
> *veh meri guru hai,*
> *Guru hai!!*

(All of a sudden that person.../Right before me/in the bylanes, on the streets, amid crowds/he is carrying on./The heart starts pounding/The mouth opens to hail him/And then suddenly.../ There he is, there he is/He's lost yet again in some public clamour.../This raised arm remains raised!!

He is the highest accomplishment of my undiscovered prosperity,/The ultimate expression .../I am his disciple/She is my master,/My master!!) [My translation.]

The "ultimate expression" is, in the poem, "that person" who suddenly appears "in bylanes and streets, and among crowds", only to disappear equally suddenly. Thus the ultimate expression, the poem speaks of, is subtraction or the unleashing of desire encountered in its evanescent eventality and thus consequent interruption in its various determinate moments or subject-positions of actuality. This is why the envisaging of this "ultimate expression"—as the determinate recommencement of subtraction for its universalisability—is always unavoidable and is, yet, forever a wager. It is not for nothing the poet says that all the risks of expression will have to be hazarded (*Abhivyakti ke saare khatre uthane hee pardenge.*).

Friendship/Comradeship: From Fraternity to Encounter

This unavoidable wager of affirming the intersubjectivity of encounter as mutual partaking of generic singularities is rearticulated by Muktibodh, to begin with, as the problematic of friendship in '*Isi Baelgadi ko*' (To this Bullock Cart) (1988, pp. 39-49):

Iske liye kya karen
tumhare hamare beech
fark aabohawa ka ki
shabdon ka abhidhaarth
ek hotey huye bhi
vyanjana-lakshana-dhwani bhinn hain
iske liye kya karen hum log!

(What can be done about this/the fact that between you and us/there is a difference of climates/that despite the same set of words/between us/their connotation-metaphoricity-sound are different/what can we people do about this!) [My translation.]

The fact of existence of two different subject-positions constitutive of two different sets of connotative, metaphorical, sonic and signifying deployment of the same set of words, stands here for the simultaneous existence of two differences and the two deployments of the two differences. The two sets of differences of deployment of the words are two particular conditions of singularities or non-relationalities that make them possible in their genericness, while the sameness of the words concerned is the condition of the universality of the singular that their simultaneity as those generic singularities stands for. Clearly, these lines, pose the question of friendship as one of universalisability of singularity: the uninterrupted simultaneity of infinite difference and infinite deployment of infinite difference.

Subsequently, the poem moves towards displacing this problematic of friendship as one of intersubjectivity of encounter, into a problematic of revolutionary solidarity of the working class amid its internally segmented situation and mutually competitive articulation within capital.

Apne dono bhai hain!!
Aur dono dukhi hain
dono hain kasht-grast

phir bhi tum lardte ho humse!!
Baelgadi ek hai
aur vahi hankna
sirf ek fark hai
fark abohawa ka.

(We are brothers!!/And both of us are unhappy/suffering is our common lot/yet you fight us!!/The bullock cart is the same/ and the same way we drive it/there is only one difference/the difference of climates) [My translation.]

Derrida (2005, p. 305) makes a rather crucial gesture in the direction of transvaluation of conceptions of fraternity and friendship when he writes: "...I have never stopped asking myself, I request that it be asked, what is meant when one says 'brother', when someone is called 'brother'. And when the humanity of man, as much as the alterity of the other, is thus resumed and subsumed. And the infinite price of friendship. I have wondered, and I ask, what one wants to say whereas one *does not want* to say , one knows that one should not say, because one knows, through so much obscurity, whence it comes and where this profoundly obscure language has led in the past. *Up until now*. I am wondering, that's all, and request that it be asked, what the implicit politics of this language is. For always, and today more than ever. What is the political impact and range of this chosen word, among other possible words, even—and especially—if the choice is not deliberate." (Emphases author's)

However, what is only a gesture in Derrida, thanks to the tentativeness of his ethical position and its deconstructive subjective orientation, is, in this poem, placed on a firmer programmatic ground. The poem sets up the resumption and subsumption of "the alterity of the other", which comes into play when "someone is called a brother", in terms of radical antagonism, and thus an asymmetrical dialectic, between two conceptions of friendship (fraternal and aggregative, and processual and constellational). These two conceptions of friendship or unity are basically those of the intersubjectivity of relationality, its constitutive structure of exchange and its materiality of social division of labour on one hand, and the intersubjectivity of encounter founding itself as its own subjective materiality of mutual partaking of generic singularities or continuous production on the other. Concomitantly, two conceptions of enmity too get posed. First is that of contradiction constitutive of a systemic unity to which people belong (and are thus friends and brothers) in and through their mutual competition and contradiction (that is, in their mutual enmity). Mutual competition, or enmity, in this instance, is the condition of being together. And all those who agree to this condition of togetherness are part of the class-divided, mutually competitive brotherhood, or fraternity, of mutual enemies. This is the fraternal realm of friendship that turns on the Schmittian axis of perpetual friend-enemy divide. In this realm, it is only in enmity, and thus in dominating and being dominated, that people can be friends. The second conception of enmity is the radical antagonism of the intersubjectivity of encounter founding itself as its own subjective materiality of relationality of the nonrelational, or continuous production, to the realm or horizon of perpetual friend/enemy divide as the intersubjectivity of relationality, its constitutive structure of exchange and its materiality of social division of labour. *'Isi Baelgadi ko'*, in posing the problematic of working-class solidarity in terms of radical antagonism between these two intersubjectivities and their respective materialities, seeks to transvalue both friendship and unity on one hand, and enmity and separation on the other.

The poem in question is clearly a critique of a conception of working-class solidarity, which even as it envisages unity of the working class to challenge capital does so by papering over the various segmentations and contradictions internal to the working class. Hence, it leaves capital, as the structure of exchange and relationality embedded within the working class, intact, and thereby reproduces capital in the very moment when it seeks to challenge it. As an articulation of this critique, the poem operates simultaneously in multiple registers (in a kind of embodied polyphony) at multiple levels of such distributive stratification or segmentation within the working class: rural and urban, peasant and worker, manual and mental, and class and its intellectual leaders. It would, therefore, not be misplaced at all to read this poem as a critique of vanguardist substitutionism as the ultimate form of social division of labour and thus capital within the working-class movement.

Kintu tum asafalta, kamjori hamari
hriday ke bhitar kee jeb kee notebook mey
jaroor aank lete ho!!
Galat karan galat sutra,
Galat srot prastut karte hueye
siddh karna chahte ho
ki hum bilkul galat hain
hamara chalna galat
galat astitva hee!!

Hum saaf keh den ki
asal mey yeh hai ki naagavar
gujarta hai tumko ki hum log
nirantar yudhmaan
jeevan ke shaashtra aur shastra hain
kyunki hum
dekhte hain anivaarya
mrityu us sabhyata kee
jiska tum jaane-anjaane nit
karte ho samarthan!!
Isliye tum hamey
sabse bade shatru samajhte ho!!

Kshama karo, tum merey bandhu aur mitra ho
Isliye sabse adhik dukhdaayee
bhayanak shatru ho.

(But our failures and weaknesses you/unfailingly assess,/in the notebook in the inner pocket of your heart!!/Presenting wrong reasons wrong formulae,/wrong sources/you want to prove/that we are completely wrong/our conduct is wrong/ wrong our very existence!!

"Let us say it loud and clear/that this is unacceptable/does it occur to you that we are/the perpetually battle-absorbed/ scriptures and weapons of life/because we/see the inevitable/ death of that civilisation/which you knowingly or unknowingly constantly/seek to support!!/That is why you consider/us your greatest adversary!!/Forgive me, you are my companion and friend/and so my most grievous/dangerous enemy.) [My translation.]

The last five lines of this stanza are particularly crucial. They demonstrate how a vanguardist conception of leadership leads to working-class solidarity being envisaged in terms of fraternal unity, which as a form of unity is constitutively segmented. What this means is the vanguardist sees himself as a friend of the class only by first envisaging the latter as an enemy to be defeated and subordinated to the substitutionist command of its leadership, and its a priori 'science' of the revolution, and thus in the process become its friend. The vanguardist thus ends up—as the poem, that is here the voice of the class, says—being the unwitting (or not) supporter of the (capitalist) civilisation whose death the working class is able to see through the everydayness of its collective experience. The class then goes on to pose itself against this vanguardist conception of class 'solidarity', constitutive of the axis of perpetual friend/enemy divide, as its radically antagonistic enemy. And in doing so it affirms a radically novel conception of friendship as subtraction from the fraternal structure of hierarchised exchange and its intersubjectivity of relationality through its disavowal and destruction. For, subtraction in tending towards its own universalisability as becoming-subtraction tends to be the intersubjectivity of encounter as mutual partaking of generic singularities, whose subjective materiality is continuous production that precludes social division of labour. What this means in practical terms is that the struggle of a subordinate segment of the working class against a dominant segment of the same—or for that matter the struggle of the class against its vanguardist-substitutionist leadership)—will not be simply negation of determination to constitute yet another determination. That would be affirmation all right, but affirmation of the structure of exchange, determination and relationality. It will not be a struggle in which the subordinate contends against the dominant either to improve its situation vis-à-vis the latter (bargaining) or to dominate the dominant. Rather, it will be a struggle of the subordinate to neutralise the countervailing force of the structure, which the dominant in being as such incarnates in the historical specificity of that dominant/subordinate relationship to prevent the former from posing the intersubjectivity of encounter or determinate abolition of social division of labour. It is such a struggle, characterised by Mao (1977, p. 91) as there being "at once unity and struggle", that is revolutionary. *Isi Baelgadi ko* (To this Bullock Cart) exemplifies the universalisability of subtraction as a transvaluation of both friendship (from fraternal to constellational) and enmity (from contradiction to radical antagonism). Victor Serge probably had such transvaluation of enmity and friendship in mind when he sought to characterise revolutionary transformation as "war without hate".

A Natural History of the Moon: When Darkness is Illumination

Ultimately, Muktibodh's politico-aesthetic quest seems to have been one that sought to rescue nature from history. His *Chand ka Muh Terdha Hai* (The Mouth of the Moon is Twisted) (1988, pp. 93-111) is the most apposite instantiation of that quest. Let us read a few lines from one of the stanzas of the poem to see if this claim can be substantiated:

> *Harijan-basti mey, mandir ke paas ek*
> *kabith ke dhard per,*
> *Mathmaeley chhaparon per,*
> *Bargad kee ainthee hueyee jar per*
> *kuhaase ke bhooton ke latke choonar ke cheethare*
> *Angiya va ghaagre, phati hueyee chadareyen*
> *Aatak gayee jinme ek*
> *vyabhichaari taktaki*
> *ganje sir, terdhe-muh chaand kee hee kanjee aankh.*

(In the shanty-town of untouchables, near the temple/on the torso of the *kabith* tree,/on the murky thatched roofs,/on the rigid roots of the banyan tree/hang the rags of stoles of foggy ghosts/and their blouses, skirts and worn-out sheets/in which is stuck the/lecherous gaze of/the bald-headed, twisted-mouthed, cock-eyed moon.) [My translation.]

The imagery articulated in these lines establishes an anthropomorphic relationship between a bald-headed, twisted-mouthed, cock-eyed moon and its lecherous gaze, and rags of women's clothing. This is, however, just one example of the anthropomorphisation of nature that the poem in the entirety of its imagery, and its animation, is an articulation of. In the light of such perversely twisted anthropomorphisation of nature that reveals the latter as unmitigatedly vicious, it ought to become rather clear that the poet's intention here is not to affirm nature as an anthropomorphic entity; an identity. Rather, the anthropomorphisation of nature, the moon in this instance, is meant to historicalise nature. It is, therefore, meant to reveal that what we perceive to be given to us as nature is actually historically determined and cathected. In this instance, the moon, appearing as a lecher on account of the smoke of capitalist industrialisation, is an image and a metaphor of the historical determination and distortion of nature in and through the simultaneity of its cathection and censoring. However, the nature that is sought to be rescued from history through such a move is not a hidden ontology of history that both determines history and is, in turn, occluded by it. For, such a rescuing of nature would only mean turning the ontological ontic, thereby once again identitarianising nature and causing it to lapse into and be conflated with the historical.

Instead, the move to rescue nature that the poem in question poses consists of disavowing nature as an identitarianised, unreflexive and thus mythical conception, which on account of such identitarianisation is therefore integral to history and its constitutive structure of exchange and relationality. Adorno writes in 'The Idea of Natural History': "The concept of nature that is sought to be dissolved is one that, if I translated it into standard philosophical terminology, would come closest to the concept of myth.... By it is meant what has always been, what as fatefully arranged predetermined being underlies history and appears in history, it is substance in history. What is delimited by these expressions is what I mean here by 'nature.'" And *Chand ka Muh Terdha Hai* (The Mouth of the Moon is Twisted) can be read as a perfect echo of this Adornoesque natural-historical project of rescuing nature from history by dissolving the mythical concept of nature as a "predetermined being that underlies history".

Adorno further writes: "If the question of the relation of nature and history is to be seriously posed, then it only offers any chance of solution if it is possible *to comprehend historical being in its most extreme historical determinacy, where it is most historical, as natural being, or if it were possible to comprehend nature as an historical being where it seems to rest most deeply in itself as nature*. It is no longer simply a matter of conceptualizing the fact of history as a natural fact *toto caelo* (inclusively) under the category of historicity, but rather to retransform the structure of inner-historical events into a structure of natural events. No being underlying or residing within historical being itself is to be understood as ontological, that is, as natural being. The retransformation of concrete history into dialectical nature is the task of the ontological reorientation of the philosophy of history: the idea of natural history." [Emphasis author's.] Following from this conception of "natural history", we see the poem reveal, through a perverse anthropomorphisation of nature, that what we perceive and know as nature in its eternal givenness is actually the historical rendered static and thus a cage. Consequently, the poem eventually also tends in the direction of a dialectical reversal—the kind which Adorno's conception of "natural history" articulates and poses—to have nature rescue itself from history by tending to disavow and destroy history in subtracting from it.

If what we perceive as nature is revealed as history then what we know as history in its dynamism is nature. Therefore, nature, in this poem, is the uninterrupted processuality of becoming-subtraction. And if subtraction *becomes* only by determinately recommencing itself in and as disavowal of its prior interruptions, nature is also determinate subtraction from the structure of exchange and relationality and is thus use-value. However, since nature as actualised subtraction is inescapably determinate it always runs the risk of being interrupted and thus lapse into an identity, which by virtue of being the manifest reality constitutive of the structure of exchange and relationality is historical. Hegel, in Volume One ('The Objective Logic'), Book Two ('The Doctrine of Essence') of his *The Science of Logic*, explicitly demonstrates that while appearance is not essence "essence must appear". It is this Hegelian dialectic that a Marxist, in approaching and intervening in reality must always bear in mind, even as he wrenches the essence free of its constitutive Hegelian horizon of identity-principle to transfigure and found it as its own ground of the real of nonidentity, obviously in radical antagonism to the principle of identity, or the law of value, it is in Hegel, or in capital in its systemic givenness, respectively. If we bear this in mind we will see, as Adorno and Muktibodh appear to do, how history is the abstraction (or ideologisation) of nature that inheres in nature – which is the determinate eruption of the Real of nonidentity—as its limit. This is the operation *Chand ka Muh Terdha Hai* (The Mouth of the Moon is Twisted) reveals and militates against.

Thus, history as identity and determination is lapsed nature, while nature in its universalisability is the uninterrupted dispersion of being-subtraction and thus what Marx called "real history" that poses no end and is always beginning. Hence nature is, as Adorno's conception of "natural history" reveals through the dialectical reversal on which it turns, the uninterrupted de-identitarianising process of perpetual dispersion. Hence, Nature, free from the historical, is nonidentity in, as and for itself. That is something Muktibodh seems to have grasped rather well. The darkness and night of much of his poetry, and its images, that he shows himself encountering and living as their authorial-subject, are not things that seek to be lit up from the outside, and thus determined and identitarianised. Rather, the dark night of his poetry, in being encountered and lived as such by their authorial-subject, has a luminosity all its own. The concluding stanza of the poem, as the history-suspending denouement it is, is a brilliantly unambiguous instantiation of this luminosity of darkness:

Samay ka kan-kan
gagan kee kaalima se
boond-boond chu raha
tardit ujala ban.

(Particles of time/drip slowly from the darkness of the sky/ transformed into/droplets of lightning illumination.)

Clearly, these "droplets of lightning illumination" comprise what ought to be called the 'light of darkness'. It is a light that dawns when our eyes get accustomed to the dark, and enables us to see without the aid of any external illumination if we dwell in darkness for long. That is akin to being darkness itself. Muktibodh can, therefore, justifiably be called the poet of darkness. That is not simply because his poetry speaks to us about darkness. Rather, we owe him such a designation because he, as the authorial-subject of his poetry, clearly speaks darkness, dwells in it and *is it*. His poetry, and he as its grammatically articulated authorial-subject, together affirm and actualise the politics of being-nonidentity.

The Restless Eagle: In Kenosis, On the Edge of Kairos

Muktibodh did not want to be a writer of poetry. He wished to be poetry itself by writing it, thereby seeking to dissolve and merge himself into the interminable process of becoming-poetry, and thus render the poetry he wrote and the politics his self embodied in its practice into one, single uninterrupted process of dispersion. Even that distributive stratification, or division of labour, between the politically militant poet, and his work, he sought to disavow. Yet he could do so, paradoxically enough, only by being the authorial-subject of *his* poetry, constrained by the finitude of the grammar of the poems he wrote, and thus confined in their time. According to Blanchot (1995, p. 117), "This contradiction is the heart of poetic experience, it is its essence and its law; there would be no poet if he did not have to live out this very impossibility, endlessly present."

Therefore, Muktibodh sought to recognise his identitarianised self—produced by the subjectivation effected by the structure of capital embodied by the society he inhabited —for the non-character, the Vipaatra (title of a novel by him) it really was. In seeking to unearth that non-characterness, which his self really was but which stood occluded in it being that individual self in its socio-historical givenness, he wished to be an incarnation of the uninterrupted process of dispersion and desubjectivation by dissolving into it. As a result, the constant evacuation of the self, or kenosis, his poetry brings into being—something that is registered, as we have earlier seen, by the epic interminability of most of his poems—is an aspiration and striving for the grace or kairos of history-suspending, "now-time" (Benjamin, 2003, p. 395). This now-time, it must be stated here, is a perpetually open, nonidentitarian, singular present—a "present without presence" (Derrida, 1994, pp. xix-xx)—that will, therefore, neither itself lapse into nor produce the identity of the past. Rosenzweig (2008, p. 289) explicates this conception of now-time with great poetic clarity and elegance when he writes: "A Today re-created into eternity must therefore in the first place correspond to this determination by an infinite Now. But an imperishable Today—is it not gone with the wind like every moment? Is it now to be imperishable? There remains but one solution: the moment which we seek must begin again at the very moment that it vanishes, it must recommence in its own disappearance, its perishing must at the same time be a reissuing." Muktibodh's poetry does not seek empowerment and progress. What it tends towards, instead, is emancipation from power and progress, and thus redemption from history that is the temporality of progress. In such circumstances, the question we need to ask is what is the politics of such poetry? More pertinently, therefore, what is politics for such poetry? The answer ought to be clear. It is the duration of redemption that such poetry institutes.

The characteristic epicality of Muktibodh's poetry—which is a registration of its kenotic being and thus its kairological aspiration and striving—is, first and foremost, the reason why it should be seen as political. For, his poetry, like "all political poetry", "pertains to the epic, which is only obliquely poetic, namely, by whatever escapes its magnificence rather than by that which brings out its splendour". (Badiou, 2009, p. 77.) The following lines from *Andherey Mey* (In the Darkness)—the most characteristic and perhaps the longest of Muktibodh's (1988, pp. 164-165) epic poems—constitute precisely such an "obliquely poetic" move:

> *Kavita mey kahne kee aadat nahin, per kah doon*
> *vartaman samaj chal nahin sakta.*
> *Poonji se jura hriday badal nahin sakta,*
> *Swaatantrya vyakti ka vaadi*
> *chhal nahin sakta mutki ke mann ko,*
> *Jan ko.*

(Not my habit to say it in a poem, let me say it nonetheless/the present society cannot go on./A heart connected to capital cannot change,/The valley of an individual's freedom/cannot deceive the soul of liberation,/the people.) [My translation.]

A hurried and casual reading of these lines might appear to suggest that the poem in question is putting itself out as a propagandist instrumentality of politics. However, a closer reading—which grasps these lines in terms of their situation within and articulation by the epical formal organisation and structural internality of the poem as a whole—would reveal that the poem intends them to be indicative of its own excess: that which "escapes its (poetic) magnificence". Poetry is clearly not politics. And yet, poetry must, in being poetry, be its own problematisation if it is to sustain itself as an affirmation of the generic singularity that it is in its determinate and paradigmatic emerging. For that, poetry, even as it remains poetry, must reflexively prefigure the overcoming of its own identitarianisation, which it tends towards on account of it being a determinate incarnation of generic singularity or subtraction in its paradigmatic emerging. Thus poetry must, precisely through its poeticness, its being-poetry, point towards politics as the excess and exceeding of its own identitarianisation. That is exactly what *Andherey Mey* (In the Darkness) seeks to do through these lines. And in doing that, the poem tends to affirm itself as the generic singularity that it is in its emerging by indicating the recommencement-for-universalisability of generic singularity in and as politics. The actuality of politics as the recommencement of the singular in its universalisability would, as we have observed earlier, amount to mutual partaking of generic singularities, including art and politics. Such universality of the singular would be constitutive of, to reiterate it here yet again, the uninterrupted process of simultaneity of infinite difference and infinite deployment of infinite difference. In such a situation, poetry becomes a generic process constitutive of politics as the actuality of universal singularity, which is the interminable process of scission or dispersion. Hence, poetry becomes political not by being a poetry of politics, or a poetry on politics, or a poetry for politics. Rather, poetry is political only when it tends to be poetry *in* politics.

The kairological aspiration and striving of Muktibodh's poetry, evident in its kenotic being, entails that the poet as the grammatical-subject of his poetry "be already what he will be later". Blanchot (1995, p. 117) writes: "...the poet must exist as a presentiment of himself, as the future of his existence. He does not exist, but he has to be already what he will be later, in a 'not yet' that constitutes the essential part of his grief, his misery, and also his great wealth...." To this he (1995, p. 118) subsequently adds: "...since it is this always-to-come existence of the poet that makes all the future possible, and firmly maintains history in the perspective of 'tomorrow' that is richer with meaning, *deutungsvoller*, and for which one must strive in the emptiness of the lived day." For Muktibodh, the grammatical authorial-subject of his poetry, politics is the future of the existence of his poetry. He, as that grammatical authorial-subject of his poetry, and that poetry itself, do not exist as politics. That is because, as we have observed, poetry as such is not politics. Nevertheless, as the aforementioned lines of *Andherey Mey* (In the Darkness) so sharply demonstrate, he makes himself and his poetry exist as their own presentiment, as the future of their existence, which, for him and his poetry, is politics.

Muktibodh's poems, therefore, constituted an evil necessity for him. They were mirage and deceptions that interrupted the journey of the dispersion of his self, if only to keep that journey going by inducing it to always recommence itself. The poet was, by his own admission, a restless eagle, the "*bechain cheel*" of his eponymous poem (1988, p. 186):

Bechain cheel!!!
Us-jaisa main paryatansheel
pyasa-pyasa,
dekhta rahoonga ek damakti hueyee jheel
ya paani ka kora jhansa
jiski safed chilchilahaton mey hai ajeeb
inkar ek soona!!

(Restless eagle!!!/Like him, I am an excursion-seeker/always thirsty/I will look out for a shining lake/or a mirage of water/in whose white shimmer there is a strange/empty denial.) [My translation.]

Gajanan Madhav Muktibodh: pessimist of the intellect, optimist of the will. The "man without qualities" of Hindi literature.

NOTES

1. Continuous production is discernibly the principle that underpinned and structured Brecht's thinking on, and practice of, theatre, literature and politics. That this principle can be conceptualised thus is indicated by Brecht in many of his theoretical writings. One of the clearest pointers in that direction

is the following entry in his *Journals: 1934-1955* (1993, p. 136): "It is however much more practical to define it [socialism] as *great production*. production must of course be taken in the broadest sense, and the aim of the struggle is to free the productivity of all men from all fetters." However, it is Brecht's (1964, pp. 183-205) detailed exposition of productivity in his 'A Short Organum for the Theatre' that leaves very little doubt on that score. Brecht (1964, p. 205), in concluding the 'Organum' by foregrounding and affirming what is clearly the principle of continuous production, impels and enables us to grasp and conceptualise the principle the way we have in this essay: "...our representations must take second place to what is represented, men's life together in society; and the pleasure felt in their perfection must be converted into the higher pleasure felt when the rules emerging from this life in society are treated as imperfect and provisional. In this way the theatre leaves its spectators productively disposed even after the spectacle is over. Let us hope that their theatre may allow them to enjoy as entertainment that terrible and never-ending labour which would ensure their maintenance, together with the terror of their unceasing transformation. Let them here produce their own lives in the simplest way; for the simplest way of living is in art."

2. The subjective in being articulated within and animated by the structure of exchange and relationality is objectified and thus idealist and not, in the final analysis, the truth and/or actuality of the subjective. Such idealism amounts to duality, wherein the subjective is no more than a competing determination whose destiny is either to determine the objective or be determined as the objective. Materialism then would be characterised by the subjective founding itself as its own materiality (subjective materiality). This being of the subjective implies preclusion of its interpellation and subjectivation, by the structure of exchange and relationality, into a competing determination that in being such a competing determination co-founds the subjectivating structure in question. Clearly, this would be the subjective being singular by becoming singular. Becoming-singular, which is becoming-subtraction from and thus antagonism to the ontological horizon or structure of exchange and relationality, is thus the uninterrupted processuality of dispersion or scission. This

uninterruptedness of the process of dispersion, which gives it its unity as such a process, is the 'relationality' among the infinitely various moments of singularisation or nonrelationality constitutive of that dispersion process. This is universalisation of the singular or being-universal-singular, which can also be termed, following Badiou, as subtractive ontology. Althusserian desubjectivation seeks to conceptualise precisely this subjective materiality of being-universal-singular or the processuality of subtractive ontology. Subjective materiality is, therefore, the uninterrupted or unlapsed continuity of the singularity of difference and deployment of difference. This conception of subjective materiality is derived in Badiou (2009, p. 189) from his argument for "a materialism centred upon a theory of the subject". The two citations below from Badiou (2009, p. 186, p. 189) should somewhat clarify this conception of "subjective materiality":

"Materialism stands in internal division to its targets. It is not inexact to see in it a pile of polemical scorn. Its internal makeup is never pacified. Materialism most often *disgusts* the subtle mind.

"The history of materialism finds the principle of its periodization in its adversary. Making a system out of nothing else than what it seeks to bring down and destroy, puffed up in latent fits of rage, this aim is barely philosophical. It gives colour, in often barbarous inflections, to the impatience of destruction....

"However, this time of offensive subjectivization produces no stability. We see this as early as in the French Revolution, when the anti-Christian excess of the provisory allies, the plebeians of the cities, is broken by Hebert's execution on the guillotine, whereas the regeneration of spiritualism of the great idealist systems connotes the possibility of a universal concordat. Bourgeois secularism, established through the State, will sometimes be anticlerical, never materialist."

"Neither God nor Man, in modern idealism, has the function of the organizer of being. The constituent function of language, which excentres every subject-effect, deactivates the materialist operator of the inversion—of the inversion in the sense in which Marx spoke of putting Hegel back on his feet.

"To claim, by a 'materialist' inversion, to go from the real to the subject means to fall short of modern dialectical criticism, which separates the two terms—subject and real—so that a third, the symbolic or discourse, comes in to operate as a nodal point without for this reason becoming a centre.

"Barred from the path of a simple inversion and summoned to hold onto the scission in which the subject of idealinguistery comes into being as an effect of the chain, we Marxists find ourselves on the dire road of a procedure of destruction-recomposition.

"To pierce through the adversary's line of defence requires this heavy ramrod whose idolatrized head bears our subjective emblems."

3. Barthes (1977, pp. 209-210) elucidates the Brechtian conception of axiomatics rather well when he writes: " 'All that is necessary', comments Brecht, 'is to determine those interpretations of facts appearing within the proletariat engaged in the class struggle (national or international) which enable it to utilize the facts for its action. They must be synthesized in order to create an axiomatic field.' Thus every fact possesses several meanings (a plurality of 'interpretations') and amongst those meanings there is one which is proletarian (or at least which is of use to the proletariat in its struggle); by connecting the various proletarian meanings one constructs a revolutionary axiomatics. But who determines the meaning? According to Brecht, the proletariat itself (*'appearing within the proletariat'*). Such a view implies that class division has its inevitable counterpart in a division of meanings and class struggle its equally inevitable counterpart in a war of meanings: so long as there is class struggle (national or international), the division of the axiomatic field will be inexpiable." (Emphasis author's)
4. The way Badiou (2005, pp. 132-133) thinks the 'relation' between destruction and the mode of subtraction, or what he alternatively also calls "newness", in an interview is instructive for our purposes and important: "I don't say in *L 'Etre et l' evenement* (*Being and Event*) that destruction is always a bad thing. It can be necessary to destroy something for the newness of the event. But I don't think it is a necessary part of newness. Because I think the newness is a supplementation and not a destruction. It is something which happens, something which comes, and this point is the crucial point. *It is possible that for the becoming of the newness something has to be destroyed* but it is not the essence, the being, the kernel of the

process. It can just be a consequence...." (My emphasis.) He subsequently goes on to clarify the issue further in the same interview: "It is always possible that destruction takes place amongst the consequences of an event. You can't always avoid destruction. It's a part of the particularity of an event, the relation between destruction and affirmation. In political events this relation is very difficult to think and control. In political events and generic processes the violence is always there because many people don't like newness. The transformation of the situation is always against some people—rich men, men in power. In political truth the relation between, on the one hand, destruction and violence, and on the other hand, affirmation and supplementation is a complex relation. I think that in *Theorie du sujet* (*Theory of the Subject*), political truth was paradigmatic for me. When I wrote 'destruction is necessary', it was because political truth was the point...."

REFERENCES

Adorno, Theodor W., 'The Idea of Natural History'. In *Telos 60* (Summer 1984), tr. Robert Hullot-Kentor (Telos Press, New York, 1984).

Badiou, Alain. 2007 January. 'Destruction, Negation, Subtraction: On Pier Paolo Pasolini'. In *The Age of Poets*, tr. and ed. Bruno Bosteels Verso, London, New York, 2014).

Badiou, Alain, 'The Autonomy of the Aesthetic Process (1965)'. In *Radical Philosophy 178* (March/April 2013), tr. Bruno Bosteels (Radical Philosophy Ltd., UK, 2013).

Badiou, Alain, *Saint Paul: The Foundation of Universalism*, tr. Ray Brassier (Stanford University Press, Stanford, California, 2003).

Badiou, Alain, *Metapolitics*, tr. Jason Barker (Verso, London, New York, 2005).

Badiou, Alain, 'An Introduction to Alain Badiou's Philosophy'. In *Infinite Thought*, trs. and eds. Oliver Feltham and Justin Clemens (Viva, Chennai, 2005).

Badiou, Alain, 'The Definition of Philosophy'. In *Infinite Thought*, trs. and eds. Oliver Feltham and Justin Clemens (Viva, Chennai, 2005).

Badiou, Alain, 'Ontology and Politics: An Interview with Alain Badiou'. In *Infinite Thought*, trs. and eds. Oliver Feltham and Justin

Clemens (Viva, Chennai, 2005).
Badiou, Alain, 'The Indissoluble Salt of Truth'. In *Theory of the Subject*, tr. Bruno Bosteels (Continuum, London, 2009).
Badiou, Alain, 'The Black Sheep of Materialism'. In *Theory of the Subject*, tr. Bruno Bosteels (Continuum, London, 2009).
Badiou, Alain, 'The Subject Under the Signifiers of the Exception'. In *Theory of the Subject*, tr. Bruno Bosteels (Continuum, London, 2009).
Badiou, Alain, 'Rhapsody for the Theatre: A Short Philosophical Treatise'. In *Rhapsody for the Theatre*, tr. and ed. Bruno Bosteels (Verso, London, New York, 2013).
Barthes, Roland, 'Writers, Intellectuals, Teachers'. In *Image Music Text*, tr. and ed. Stephen Heath (Fontana Press, London, 1977).
Bataille, Georges, *The Accursed Share*, Volume I, tr. Robert Hurley (Zone Books, New York, 1998).
Benjamin, Walter, 'On the Concept of History'. In *Selected Writings* (Volume 4), tr. Edmund Jephcott and Others, eds. Marcus Bullock, Howard Eiland and Michael W. Jennings (The Belknap Press of Harvard University Press, Cambridge, Massachusetts, 2006).
Blanchot, Maurice, 'The Essential Solitude'. In *The Space of Literature*, tr. Ann Smock (University of Nebraska Press, Lincoln, London, 1989).
Blanchot, Maurice, 'The "Sacred" Speech of Hoelderlin'. In *The Work of Fire*, tr. Charlotte Mandell (Stanford University Press, Stanford, California, 1995).
Bosteels, Bruno, 'Translator's Introduction'. In Alain Badiou, *Theory of the Subject*, tr. Bruno Bosteels (Continuum, London, 2009).
Brecht, Bertolt, *Journals: 1934-1955*, tr. Hugh Rorrison, ed. John Willet (Methuen, London, 1993).
Brecht, Bertolt, 'A Short Organum for the Theatre'. In *Brecht on Theatre: The Development of an Aesthetic*, tr. and ed. John Willet (Hill and Wang, New York, 1964).
Derrida, Jacques, *The Politics of Friendship*, tr. George Collins (Verso, London, New York, 2005).
Derrida, Jacques, *Spectres of Marx*, tr. Peggy Kamuf (Routledge, London, 1994).
Jameson, Fredric, *Brecht and Method* (Verso, London, New York, 2000)
Lefebvre, Henri, *Critique of Everyday Life, Volume I*, tr. John Moore (Verso, London, New York, 1992).
Mao, Tsetung, 'On the Correct Handling of Contradictions Among

the People'. In *Five Essays on Philosophy* (Foreign Language Press, Peking, 1977).

Marx, Karl, 'Preface'. In *A Contribution to the Critique of Political Economy*, tr. S.W. Ryazanskaya, ed. Maurice Dobb (Progress Publishers, Moscow, 1984).

Marx, Karl, *Capital: A Critique of Political Economy, Volume I*, trs. Samuel Moore and Edward Aveling, ed. Fredrick Engels (Progress Publishers, Moscow, 1986).

Muktibodh, Gajanan Madhav, *Ek Sahityik ki Diary* [Diary of a Litterateur] (Bhartiya Gyanpeeth, New Delhi, 2002).

Muktibodh, Gajanan Madhav, *Pratinidhi Kavitayen* [Representative Poems], ed. Ashok Vajpeyi (Rajkamal Paperbacks, New Delhi, 1988).

Negri, Antonio, *The Labour of Job*, tr. Matteo Mandarini (Duke University Press, Durham & London, 2009).

Parsai, Harishankar, 'Muktibodh: Ek Sansmaran' [Muktibodh: A Memoir]. In *Premchand ke Phatey Jootey* [Premchand's Worn-out Shoes], ed. Gyan Ranjan (Bhartiya Gyanpeeth, New Delhi, 2011).

Rosenzweig, Franz, *The Star of Redemption*, tr. William W. Hallo (University of Notre Dame Press, Notre Dame, 2008).